The
Dreamer's
COMPANION

The
Dreamer's

COMPANION

A YOUNG PERSON'S GUIDE TO UNDERSTANDING
DREAMS AND USING THEM CREATIVELY

Stephen Phillip Policoff

Library of Congress Cataloging-in-Publication Data
Policoff, Stephen Phillip.
   The dreamer's companion : a young person's guide to understanding
dreams and using them creatively / Stephen Phillip Policoff.
      p.   cm.
   Includes bibliographical references.
   ISBN 1-55652-280-0
      1. Dreams.   I. Title.
BF1091.P65 1997
154.6'3-dc21   97-10256
                                                     CIP

©1997 by Stephen Phillip Policoff
All rights reserved
First edition
Published by Chicago Review Press, Incorporated
814 North Franklin Street
Chicago, Illinois 60610
ISBN 1-55652-280-0
Printed in the United States of America
5

for Kate

"So, I wasn't dreaming after all . . . unless . . .
unless we're all part of the same dream. Only I
do hope it's my dream. . . . I don't like belonging
to another person's dream."

—*Alice in Wonderland*

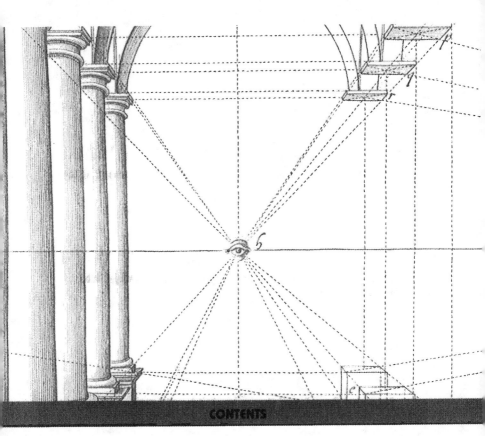

CONTENTS

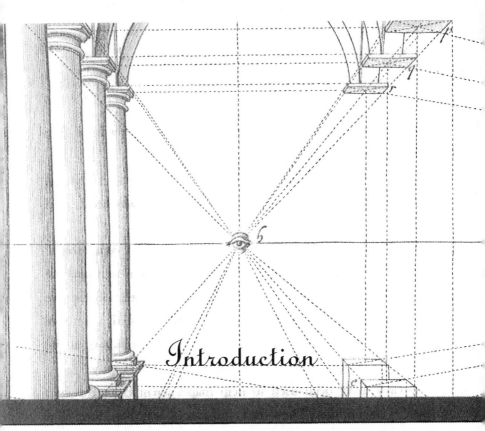

Introduction

The ancient Chinese philosopher Chuang-Tzu dreamed one night that he was a butterfly. When he awoke, he confided in his journal that he would never again be sure if he were a man dreaming he was a butterfly or a butterfly dreaming he was a man. Dreams are often like that—absurd, haunting, fascinating, sometimes even life-altering.

During our lifetime, we will spend approximately four years in a dream state, but in modern American society, many people still consider the study of dreams to be something only New Age weirdos would pursue.

They are wrong. Dreams have inspired scientists, composers, and presidents. Dreams can cause us to laugh, shudder, create, and learn.

We shouldn't be surprised that dreams remain a controversial subject. They have been called both a gift from heaven *and* the work of the devil! The twisted stories, images, and relationships we see in our sleep have been both feared and ridiculed; they have been thought of as a disgusting by-product of the mind and as the secret pathway to self-understanding.

Dreams have been used to help map ancient conquests and modern inventions. They have influenced art, literature, and music. Even television and popular songs have fallen under the magical sway of dreams—how many silly situation comedies can you think of that have featured dream sequences, and how many hundreds of pop songs have the word "dream" in them?

Virtually every ancient culture had men and women whose task it was to act as dream interpreters: priests and priestesses, shamans, oracles, and prophets. The Bible is full of dreams, and so is almost every collection of ancient wisdom we possess.

In our own era, psychologists and psychiatrists seem to have taken over the job of dream interpretation, but poets and film-makers and ordinary people have also been active in transforming the mysterious world of dreams into a rich language that enhances our wide-awake life.

The Russian-American author Vladimir Nabokov once observed that "reality" is the only word that makes no sense unless enclosed in quotation marks. What is real? What is illusion? Can we leap in time and space? Is each individual human mind part of some larger universal mind? Dreams help illuminate these *Twilight Zone* questions better, perhaps, than any other element of our lives.

This book is meant to help thrust open a window for you, a window that looks out onto this mysterious realm. It will offer you a glance at some of the ways in which dreams have been understood in the past and the amazing strides forward science has recently made in understanding the dream state.

It will, I hope, guide you in your quest to make some sense of your dreams, help you use them as building blocks for creative projects, and offer you access to that fleeting landscape of the beautiful and the weird.

This book came about because of my own interest in dreams, the pleasure I have taken in them, the creative work that has flowed from them, and the wonder and excitement I have seen in my students as they were dragged—some kicking and screaming!—into exploring the *Alice in Wonderland* world of their own dreams.

I have used dreams as a route for teaching writing to students from ages twelve to sixty-five (not at the same time, though!), and I have often been amazed at the profound, luminous, and downright off-the-wall material they have produced when mining the rich vein of dream imagery. Many of my students had no particular interest in this area of study before I bludgeoned them into it, but they seemed to take to it like fledglings take to flight.

Maybe, just maybe, you'll soar upward as well.

When I set out to write this book, I wanted to include as much material as I could on the immensely complex puzzle of dream studies, so there are pieces of the puzzle I've pulled from anthropology, neurochemistry, art, and even the occult!

I wanted to give voice to experts, certainly, but I wanted something else, as well. I wanted there to be room (and a lot of it!) in this book for the voices of people a bit more like you (yes, *you*).

So, I forced, begged, cajoled, and wheedled dream observations from my students, my former students, and just about anyone else who would listen to me. Many of these dreamers were in my writing classes at the Center for Creative Youth at Wesleyan University, where I used to teach, or at New York University, where I am currently teaching. Most were between the ages of sixteen and twenty-one, though a few were my students some years ago and are now adults.

I am very much indebted to all of them for sharing their dream worlds with me, and thus with you.

A few of them felt uncomfortable being quoted in this book and asked me to alter their names, which I have done. I have also edited, slightly, some of their numerous comments, adding or subtracting a few words for sense, length, and flow.

But the comments are true—and truly remarkable—offering a series of dream snapshots, depictions of an inner life that you might find eerie, ugly, beautiful, and even faintly familiar.

In Shakespeare's *The Tempest*, the man-beast Caliban says, "when I waked, I cried to dream again." Our dreams sometimes seem so much richer than our real lives that we might indeed wish we could dream more and be awake less. But seeing our dreams for what they are may let us have the best of both worlds, capturing the richness of the house of our unconscious to help furnish the more mundane rooms of our waking life.

I hope that this book helps you to dream again and again and to see your dreams more clearly and even yourself a little more clearly.

The Unique World of the Dreamer

You possess something that is uniquely and completely your own, something that is not at all like what your parents have, your friends have, or your brother has.

This thing isn't an object, like a piece of clothing or a ring; it's smaller and infinitely more valuable. And it's not a body part, exactly. This thing you have, which is yours and yours alone, is quite mysterious, quite marvelous, and even quite useful.

OK, you might have a ring that's not like anyone else's ring that

1

you know of, but somewhere, someone has a ring just like that ring. Sure, sure, your fingerprints are unique—no one has fingerprints quite like your fingerprints—but fingerprints are only a little bit marvelous, and unless you're a detective, they're not all that useful.

This thing I'm talking about can't really be touched, can't really be measured, and unless you tell someone about it, it can't even be imagined by anyone else.

It's your dreamworld.

You enter this unique, mysterious, and marvelous world every night, several times a night. You might not think you do, but you do. Sometimes, this alternate world is just a fleeting wisp of a memory when you awaken, a fragment of a tune, a color, a feeling. Sometimes, though, it lingers on into your waking world, even when you wish it wouldn't. And sometimes, the dreamworld turns your waking world upside down and fills your night with weirdness.

This secret world that is all your own might make you laugh because it seems so absurd. It might make you shudder because it reminds you of things you aren't certain you want to remember.

And almost certainly, it has made you sit up in bed, relieved and murmuring, "Oh! That was only a dream! I am so glad that was only a dream!" Or it's made you wake up a bit sad because the things you saw and felt were so lovely and colorful and inviting in a way that the real world sometimes is not.

But however your dreamworld makes you feel—and probably it has made you feel a little like all of these—it's your world, a world that no one can enter without your permission and that no one has better insight into than you do. Your dreamworld is a world just waiting for you to explore, to learn from, to laugh about, a world that will sometimes cause you to smile quietly in understanding or scratch your head in wonderment.

And it's not like anyone else's dreamworld. No, really.

"Doesn't everybody have the same kind of dreams?" you may be wondering. For example, "I'm trying to run but my feet are frozen. I can't move. Help!"

It's true that there are so-called common dreams, situations and images that seem to appear in the dreams of all human beings throughout the world, throughout history. Carl Jung, the great psychologist and dream theorist, called these recurring images "archetypes."

So, your dreamworld might have some images, stories, patterns that are like other people's—dream archetypes—such as a dream in which you are being chased by a monster or beast. Almost everyone has had a dream at some point, usually in childhood, like these:

"When I was younger, I used to dream all the time about being chased through a labyrinth by monsters and dwarfs."
—Kate Soukhapalov

"I dreamed that Chucky from *Child's Play*, with blond hair, was chasing my family down a hallway."
—Desiree Seguritan

"I was being chased by a generic-looking dinosaur, only it was blue, and I had the feeling that the dinosaur had already gotten me."
—Lyndee Yamshon

But even when the *pattern* of a dream is a common one (monsters, hallway), the details are personal and specific (dwarfs, blue dinosaurs, Chucky). They're yours and yours alone, and they speak to you in a way that they don't speak to anyone else.

Take the being-chased-by-monsters dream. What does the monster look like in your version of this common dream? How close does the monster get to you in the dream? How do you feel as the monster approaches you? What do you do? Run? Cower?

Try to fight? Fly through the air away from the monster? Does the monster seem familiar to you, like something or someone you've seen before? At what point in this archetypal scene do you wake up?

You may not know the answers to those questions—maybe you're not even sure you care about the answers. But the ways in which your being-chased-by-monsters dream differs from your best friend's being-chased-by-monsters dream are the ways in which your dreams embody you.

Maybe the monster reflects something you were afraid of when you were a child, a part of your personality that you didn't like, a fantasy you had, or even just an image from a scary movie that is embedded in your memory.

But it's your monster, and no one can tell you what it means better than you can. This is one of the most marvelous things about exploring the dreamworld: your dreams are like a theater in which you play all the parts. You get to act out the dramas, watch them, and even write the reviews.

> *"In dreams, we see ourselves naked and acting out our real characters even more clearly than we see others awake."*
> —*Henry David Thoreau*

"So what?" you may be muttering.

That's a good question. There are plenty of people who think that spending even one moment contemplating your dreams is one moment too many. The Nobel Prize–winning biologist Sir Francis Crick suggested that trying to remember dreams was a bad idea since it might encourage us to recall images and memories our brains would be better off forgetting. Other people have suggested that dreams are like the waste product of the mind.

Probably, though, you're not one of those people, or you wouldn't be reading this book.

Probably, you feel drawn to your dreamworld on some level, intrigued, wanting to know more. Probably, when you think about it, you might agree with Jung, who called dreams "a little hidden door." Probably, you'd like to push that door open just a bit and peer inside. So, that's what we're going to do.

First Dream It—Then Do It

Let your thoughts ramble a little about your dreams. Do you often remember them, or only once in a while? How do they usually make you feel? Uneasy? Amused? Reflective? Confused?

Write a few lines down in a journal (or on your laptop, or speak into a tape recorder) in which you express your general feelings about your dreams. Here are some examples to get a flavor of this activity.

"My dreams sometimes make me laugh. The weirdest things happen, and I wonder, 'Where did that come from?'"

—Desiree Seguritan

"I almost always remember my dreams, but only in bits and pieces. Some of them are really funny, like when I met my new English aunt at Thanksgiving. That night everyone in my dreams was speaking with an English accent."

—Molly Lucier

"I've had dreams that made me joyful, angry, melancholy, fearful, hopeful, jealous, ecstatic. They usually in some way reflect my conscious being."

—Glenn Williams

7

"When I remember my dreams, I know they are important, they're trying to tell me something. They're often warnings or 'wake-up calls' about things that are happening in my life."

—Lyndee Yamshon

———✦———

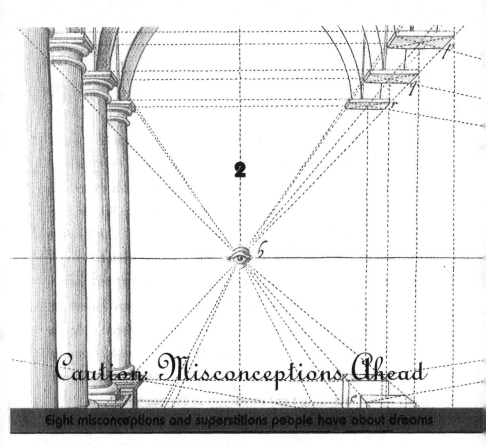

Caution: Misconceptions Ahead

We're going to be strolling through the *Alice in Wonderland* world of dreams together for quite a while, so we might as well be sure we understand each other.

I don't want to let you down, so I'll admit this right now: this book isn't going to tell you everything you want to know about your dreams. It may even tell you some things you don't want to know, that you don't agree with, or that you find downright unpleasant.

Dreams don't often go the way we wish they would go, and sometimes they're confusing and contradictory and even kind of disgusting—just like life. So, talking (or writing) about them is as complicated as talking about other difficult subjects, like sex, like politics, like why your parents argue all the time, or like why your friends sometimes don't act like they're really your friends.

And honest and intelligent people can have completely different views on these subjects and on dreams, too. Dreams have been considered both divine and demonic; dreamers have been hailed as prophets and burned as witches. So, don't be surprised if some of the ideas about dreams in this book and some of the people quoted in this book (including me!) strike you as off-the-wall.

The most important thing to remember is that you are the dream explorer here. This book isn't going to tell you everything you want to know, but it's also not going to try to tell you what to think about your dreams— that's not my job! And it's not going to sit you down and say, "This is what you were really

> *"I dreamt I dwelt in marble halls*
>
> *And each damp thing that creeps and crawls*
>
> *Went wobble-wobble on the walls."*
>
> *—Lewis Carroll*

dreaming about." Because I don't know what your dreams mean any more than you do.

But I do know a bit more about how dreams work and what some famous (and not-so-famous) thinkers have thought about dreaming, and maybe this will help you to think about your own dreams. I know, too, how to appreciate dreams, how to mine them for creative ore, and how to put them into a context, which may help you make sense of them (or laugh or marvel at them).

I've used dreams in my own writing quite often, and, at various stages of my life, I've kept a dream journal and consulted it for self-understanding as well as creative fodder. And I've used dreams to teach my writing classes for years. Yes, I have forced hundreds of unsuspecting students of all ages to do many of the things I'm going to ask you to do.

Over the next eighteen chapters, we'll look at how dreams have been perceived at other times in history and how different cultures made use of their dreams for prophecy, self-understanding, art, and fun.

But before we do that, we should get a few facts straight. There are a lot of weird ideas about dreams floating around, so let's check out a few of them.

Eight Misconceptions and Superstitions People Have about Dreams

1. *I never dream.*

   You may say this, but you don't really mean it, because if
   you never dreamed, how would you know what a dream
   was? What you probably mean is that you don't remember
   your dreams, but if you keep getting asked, you'll probably
   admit that you remember some fragment of some dream,
   usually from childhood. Dreaming is a universal condition,
   occurring during certain phases of the sleep cycle every
   night.

2. *I dream only once a night.*

   How do you know? More likely, you only remember one
   dream a night—probably the one closest to awakening.
   You enter the "REM," or rapid eye movement, stage of
   sleep about four or five times every night; that's when most
   dreams occur (we'll talk about this again later). Since each
   dream may actually be a series of linked fragments, the
   number of dreams could be quite vast, but you are likely to
   have at least four dreams during any given night.

3. *I'm incapable of remembering my dreams.*

   More likely, you haven't tried very hard, you aren't getting a lot of sleep, or else you're drinking a great deal of alcohol, which would be alarming. Certainly, there are people who have a harder time remembering their dreams than others, and everyone goes through periods when they're not remembering their dreams. But if you work at it (more about this later!), you can and will remember your dreams.

4. *If you die in your dream, you'll die in real life.*

OK, why? This is one of those superstitions that doesn't make any sense. How would we know if it were true, anyway? We'd have to ask every dying person if they dreamed of their death the previous night. Probably a few of them did—would that be a big surprise? But they're not dying because they dreamed about dying; more likely, they dreamed about dying because they knew they were dying. Dreams sometimes seem to predict events (more about this later, too!) but there is no formula saying that if you dream about something then it will happen. Any book that tries to make dreams behave like mathematical equations is wrong or silly or a cheat.

5. *Dreams are just about sex.*

This is one of those ideas that people get when they have heard about dream theories but haven't actually read any. If you say this, you are probably thinking of Sigmund Freud (yes, more about him later, too!), the famous founder of modern psychiatry. Freud believed that dreams very often contain buried sexual symbols and that the emotional difficulties of adulthood could sometimes be resolved by unearthing these buried sexual symbols. But many dream theorists are skeptical of this idea, and even Freud never said that dreams are only about sex. Sexual fantasies, fears, and wishes sometimes appear in dreams—it would be pretty astonishing if they didn't—but dreams are not all about or only about anything.

6. *Telling someone your dreams will just show him how messed up you are!*

This assumes that you're messed up (well, maybe you are, but that's none of my business). Dreams aren't messages in secret code that someone can decode and say "Aha! Your dream about being strapped into a chair and forced to watch Arnold Schwarzenegger movies means you want to kill your history teacher." Telling someone your dreams is a tricky business, though, because dreams are both private and not-so-private, and a lot of people have preconceived ideas about them. So, just as you wouldn't read your diary aloud to anyone, you need to be careful about how and with whom you share your dream life (OK, you guessed it; we'll talk about this more later on, in the section about forming a dream group).

7. *Dreams never did anyone any good.*

Usually, when people say things like this they mean that worrying about the strange and sometimes frightening world of dream images is a waste of time. And if you think so, that's OK. No one should be forced to think about their dreams. But dreams inspired Mary Shelley to write *Frankenstein*, they inspired Robert Louis Stevenson to write *The Strange Case of Dr. Jekyll and Mr. Hyde*, they inspired the World War II hero General George Patton to attack Nazi forces by night, they inspired the German chemist Friedrich Kekule to solve the riddle of the molecular structure of benzene, and they inspired Dimitri Mendelyev to create the periodic table of the elements. And dreams have shown the way out of innumerable personal dilemmas, pointing thousands of people just like you in intriguing new directions. So, after you've read this book, you decide for yourself if thinking about dreams is a waste of time!

8. *Dreams aren't real anyway!*

This is just another way of shrugging off something you don't understand. It's like saying, "Books aren't real, so why bother to read?" or "Music isn't what life's about, so why bother to listen?" But books are real; you can hold them in your hands and feel them. And though the stories they contain may not actually have happened, they tell us things about the world that traveling around in your car will never tell you, just as music informs us about how life feels far better than any conversation. The pioneering psychologist Havelock Ellis said, "Dreams are real while they last; can we say more about life?"

First Dream It—Then Do It

Try to remember some of the things you may have heard or read about dreams. They might be odd ideas someone in your family had about dreams (my grandmother once told me that if you dreamed of sneezing, you would wake up with a cold—silly or what?) or even something you may have read or seen in school (like the biblical story of Joseph, who interpreted a pharaoh's dreams—yes, more about him later!). Here is a random sampling of some other odd ideas about dreams that people have heard, read, or imagined.

"Just staring at someone who's asleep almost guarantees he or she will dream about you."
—Adriane Vawter

"My mother uses Greek folklore to tell me about dreams. She said that if you dream something red, worries are on the way."
—Asmina Pertesis

"I've heard it said that a cheating girlfriend in a dream is really cheating on you."
—Michael Housepian

"If you dream about insects, you'll be wealthy."
—Michelle Martinez

"If the first thing you see when you wake up is a window, you'll remember your dream."
—Sarah Sherman

"If a woman dreams about water, she's about to get her period."
—Lauren Ohayon

"If you dream about falling, it means you're growing."
—Tim Shayakhmetov

Why do you think so many people have such different beliefs about dreams? Maybe we'll figure that out in the next eighteen chapters.

3

Asclepius, Joseph, and Other Heavy Dudes

1. Do dreams predict the future?

2. Do dreams come to us like a whisper in our ears, from some outside voice?

3. What should we do with people who say they can interpret our dreams?

If I asked you those questions today, you might say:

1. "Maybe."

2. "Gee, I don't know."

3. "Run away from them."

Or maybe you would just run away from me.

But in most ancient societies, there were very serious answers to those questions:

1. Not only can dreams predict the future, but that's one of their main functions.

2. Dreams are voices—of God, or the gods, or our ancestors, or spirit guides, or the devil.

3. We should give people who can interpret dreams respect, awe, fear, power . . . and maybe then we should run away from them.

Dreams were taken very seriously in virtually every ancient culture that left us written records. All of the great religions are filled with dreams and interpretations of dreams. Jacob, in the Bible's Old Testament, dreamed of a ladder ascending to the sky, demonstrating the link between God and Jacob's offspring. Muhammad, the founder of Islam, dreamed that he had been called to found a new religion and dreamed whole passages of the Moslem holy book called the Koran. In the Bible's New Testament, Joseph discovered the true nature of Mary's pregnancy in a dream and was later warned in a dream that his family must flee to Egypt to escape death.

The young Prince Gautama, who later became Buddha, dreamed of his future as a wandering monk. There is even a long section in the ancient Hindu holy scriptures called the Vedas that discusses dream interpretation and the nature of dreams.

Religion and dreams are intertwined; it's hard to imagine the one without the other. They both offer comfort and fear, and they both help to explain and add mystery to human experience.

In the ancient world that produced all these religions, dreams were looked at as an alternate way of understanding the world, like a book in a different language, and the men and women who could read that book were often the most awe-inspiring and powerful members of the community—the priests and priestesses, witches and sorcerers, wise men and oracles.

What kind of advice did these dream readers offer? They said, mostly, that dreams must be regarded as omens, messages, or warnings. These sages told kings that dreams must be taken seriously or their kingdoms might perish. They told their people that dream symbols affect us in the waking world.

There is a famous document called Chester Beatty Papyrus III, which comes from ancient Egypt. But even though it's about

4,500 years old, this document isn't so different from the little booklets you might find at the checkout counter of your local supermarket. It's a fragment of the very first guide to dream interpretation. It says that if you dream about your fingernails being removed, it means work is going to be taken away from you and if you dream of being naked, you will become an orphan. It also says that you can free yourself from a bad dream by rubbing herbs, beer, and myrrh on your face (don't try this at home!).

Even 4,500 years ago, people worried about their bad dreams and sought remedies for the anxiety they produced. And they also had elaborate ways of bringing on good dreams, of helping the dreamer to have the dream he or she wanted.

The ancient Greeks asked Asclepius, the god of healing, to visit them in their dreams and soothe them and cure them of their ills. And sometimes, he came through—but only if they performed the correct rituals.

If you were an ancient Greek who wanted to experience a visit from this dream god, you had to take the journey to one of the many temples dedicated to Asclepius. You had to refrain from sex, eat no meat, take a lot of cold baths, listen to prayers and chants, and watch as incense and fires burned through the night. You had to hang out in a temple with a lot of other would-be dreamers, priests who would whisper encouraging words to you, and snakes that slithered around on the temple floor (Asclepius liked snakes; don't ask me why).

Eventually, if all went well, you would have a dream in which Asclepius would show up and tell you what medicine to take or what acts to perform to make your life better. Sometimes, you'd have to ask the priest to interpret the dream, other times, you'd be able to figure it out for yourself.

Does that sound strange?

It isn't really so different from going to the therapist and spending an hour a week trying to make sense of your dreams or buying a book and reading it to try to make sense of your dreams.

OK, we don't have snakes slithering around now, but our contemporary perception of dreams is not so very different from the ancient Greeks'—we still look for meanings to unearth and we still hold out the possibility of life-altering insight. And while our culture as a whole does not value dreams the way the ancient world did, there are many sages still among us who say that much of the truth about human experience can be found in dreams. And the whole contemporary theory of dream incubation (see Chapter 14), owes a lot to ancient rituals like those of Asclepius.

Why is this worth knowing? Because the history of dreaming is pretty interesting in itself, but also because it makes us think about the ways we look at dreams today and how some things about the world never change at all, even over thousands of years, while other things change every other decade or so.

Take the Bible's Old Testament story of Joseph. Maybe you know how it goes. Joseph's brothers sell him into slavery in Egypt because they are jealous of him, in part because of his extraordinary dreams. In Egypt, he is falsely accused of wrongdoing and winds up in a prison. While there, he correctly interprets the dreams of two of the Pharaoh's servants who have displeased the Pharaoh and wound up in prison themselves. (Egypt wasn't a terribly fun place back then.)

When one of these servants is sprung from prison (as Joseph predicted), he hears the Pharaoh speaking of his own unsettling dreams, dreams that no one can interpret. This servant tells the Pharaoh that the best dream interpreter in the land resides in the Pharaoh's own prison, so Joseph is brought before the Pharaoh.

The Pharaoh has dreamed that seven fat cows came up out of the Nile followed by seven skinny, nasty-looking cows, who ate the seven fat cows. He also has dreamed that seven plump stalks of grain were growing on one stalk and then seven shriveled-up stalks of grain grew and swallowed up the fat stalks.

Joseph says, "That's easy! There are going to be seven fat years followed by seven lean years. If you're smart, you'll deal with this now and store food from the seven fat years for the seven skinny, nasty years to follow."

The Pharaoh is so impressed that he makes Joseph into a sort of prime minister of Egypt and gives him the authority to take care of this problem. Joseph does such a good job that his brothers show up during the famine years, begging for food. And he gives it to them, they make up, the whole family is reconciled, and it's all very sweet.

The Bible says that it is God who gives Joseph the interpretation of Pharaoh's dreams and thus provides Joseph with the means to achieve success, because he is filled with the spirit of the Lord.

But whether you want to say it's the voice of God or some intuitive sense of the mystery of the world, Joseph is clearly in tune with something other than the day-to-day concerns of life. He knows that there is strange wisdom and power in dreams, and he manages to turn his life around because he listens to that voice, which today we might call the 'unconscious,' the voice that whispers to us while we are asleep.

Joseph hears the music, the poetry, the wisdom that lives *inside*, which we often neglect because we are so busy coping with all the problems *outside.*

That may not be exactly the lesson the Bible was aiming at, but it rings true, I think, for us today. We can be misunderstood by our families, pushed around by our siblings, even falsely accused of wrongdoing, but if we remain aware that there is another important aspect of life—our inner life, our dreamworld—we may still be able to do things others can't do, see possibilities others can't see, and maybe, just maybe, we'll triumph in the end.

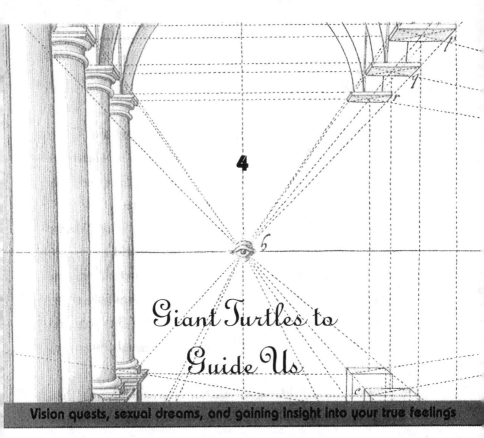

4

Giant Turtles to Guide Us

Vision quests, sexual dreams, and gaining insight into your true feelings

$\mathcal{H}$ ave you ever wished that someone—not your parents, not your homeroom teacher, not your older brother—would tell you what you should do with your life?

This person would have to be wise, would maybe have to be a little mysterious, and would have to treat you as if you were special, as if what you did with your life really mattered to the world.

Who wouldn't want such a guide?

In fairy tales and myths, there are guides like this all over the place—fairy godmothers, talking bears, benevolent wizards. They offer advice; sometimes they even hand out magical objects or words of power that help transform the poor, lost girls and boys into the heroines and heroes of their very own quests.

Why isn't there somebody like that in our real lives? Maybe there is. Maybe such a being lurks in your dreamworld.

Well, maybe not in your dreamworld, but Native Americans believed there were such beings—old men, talking animals, shadowy creatures who spoke with voices like thunder. They saw and heard these beings in their dreams and often learned from them what paths they were to take in life.

That doesn't mean, of course, that all Native Americans had such dreams or thought alike about this or anything else. Native American culture was vast and multifaceted. It spanned the whole American continent, and different tribes had tremendously different rituals, beliefs, and ways of seeing the world, both the dreamworld and the awake world.

But like the cultures of ancient Greece and Egypt, Native American culture overwhelmingly saw the dreamworld as deeply connected to the other world, the one in which we are (more or less) awake.

The Yumans, for example, from the plains of the Southwest, believed that dreams were the most significant aspect of life, that all power in life derived from dreams, that if a man had skill or strength, he had obtained it in his dreams.

The Iroquois believed that if you dreamed of giving a feast, you had to give one when you awoke because the dream expressed a wish of the soul that must not be thwarted or danger awaited. The Cherokee believed that if you dreamed you were bitten by a snake, you must treat the bite when you awoke or you might die.

You might say that for Native Americans, as for many traditional cultures around the world, the door between the world of the unconscious and the waking world was pushed open quite a bit more than it is in our own culture.

And many Native American people believed in what is called the "vision quest." That's where the wise and strange figures come in.

The vision quest usually took place in adolescence—so, maybe this would be a good time for you to learn about it! It was one of the ways in which boys achieved manhood and discovered what they would do with their lives and what kind of role they would play in their community.

But just because it was once really only for boys doesn't mean that girls can't learn from it, too. A lot of things were just for boys in a different time and place and are no longer. Dreams do not withhold power and self-knowledge because of gender!

What was a vision quest like? First, the boy was required to take a journey away from his family to a place thought to be sacred or dangerous, or on the edge of the familiar world. There, he would fast and pray; he would ask the spirits (or his ancestors) to send him a spirit guardian. He might even perform some violent physical act like cutting himself on the groin or slicing off a fingertip to help bring on the vision ("How like a boy!" some of you might be thinking).

He might drink or eat herbs that would induce visions. He might dance in a circle or position himself in a dangerous spot, like lying head downward over the edge of a cliff. And eventually he would sleep, or be uncertain if he was awake or asleep, and in this state he would have a dream. In this dream there would be a voice, a figure, or someone telling him what to do.

It might be his long-dead grandfather or a great warrior or sorcerer whom he had heard about in tribal lore. It might be a creature who held symbolic power in the tribe: a giant turtle, a wolf, or a raven. The boy might be told to await more dreams, or he might be sent to find a certain magical stone or twig to keep with him always. He might dream a protective song and then return later to this sacred spot and sing the song whenever he felt fearful or needed guidance.

When he staggered home after this exciting vision quest, he might tell his parents or the wise man of the tribe, and perhaps his dream would be told and retold throughout the village, or, depending on the tribe, he might never tell the dream because it was his alone and to tell it would be to weaken the power it had on his life.

But the dream would stay with him and would be considered one of the most important moments of his life no matter what happened to him in the future.

The great scholar of mythology Joseph Campbell once said, "Myths are public dreams; dreams are private myths." And these visions in which young people on the brink of adulthood learned some truth about their lives are both myths and dreams, and we can learn something about our own lives by thinking about them.

Like what? For one thing, we can learn about the way that our inner life and the "outside" world we are born into are inextricably bound together.

You might be wondering how these boys all managed to have such important dreams in which figures from tribal lore spoke directly to them. Were they for real? Did all the boys have the visions they claimed to have? Why didn't they ever have silly dreams, the way we often do?

They probably did. But those dreams weren't the dreams they had been sent to have, so they paid no attention to them.

We can't possibly know, of course, if the boys ever made up the dreams, but wouldn't it be surprising if this never happened? There are always people who will lie when something important is at stake.

But more than likely, most of these boys trembling on the brink of adulthood didn't really have to make up the dream in the same way that the ancient Greeks didn't have to make up a dream in which Asclepius came to them in the temple. They dreamed these things because it was important that they dream them. They were expected to dream them and they had been told they would dream them, so they did.

A vision quest is what anthropologists call a "cultural pattern dream," a dream that fits the way a particular culture sees itself and is full of the beliefs and values that form the core of that society.

In our own culture, sexual dreams or dreams in which we do battle with our parents or other authority figures might be said to fit the same kind of pattern. No one would be surprised if you reported such a dream because they fit the pattern of what is expected of young people in our society. And no one takes them very seriously, either, because dreams still carry little weight in our culture.

But if you woke up one morning and reported to your folks that you had dreamed your long-dead great-uncle came to you as a giant turtle and told you to become a healer, they would probably smile at you a little funny, drink their coffee, and dash to the phone to call your doctor. That wouldn't fit the pattern of what is expected in our culture.

Sure, you could tell them that you dreamed about your great-uncle. They might think it was odd, but after all, it is understood in our culture that we dream of people who have been important to us and that we can even learn from our dream-memories of these special people.

You could tell them there was a giant turtle in your dream, and they'd probably think you were an imaginative youth, which might make them smile to themselves, because imagination is, at least in some homes, still considered a valuable personal asset.

You could tell them that you had dreamed you were going to be a doctor, and they might even think that showed great ambition. But put all these images together and assert that they meant something important—a turning point in your life—and you would probably get a very different reaction!

Our culture, for the most part, is uncomfortable with the idea of visions and the idea that truth can come in a form different from a mathematical equation or a historical fact. You would not be rewarded with praise and power if you showed up at home with such a tale.

But to the Native American boy, such a tale would fit in well with all the tales he had ever been told of truth and power in his community. He would probably be rewarded with honor and prestige, and members of the tribe might seek him out for magic, for healing, or insight into the meaning of their own dreams.

But just because your folks aren't going to throw a huge party for you if you start having colorful, imaginative dreams doesn't mean you can't learn and gain something important from the ideas about dreams that the vision quest represents.

Dream scholar Patricia Garfield says, "You can provide yourself with the rewards for dreaming our society does not give. Regard your own dreams as important and they will aid you."

Cultural pattern dreams show us that if we expect to gain insight from our dreams, we will. If we reinforce for ourselves the idea that the figures in our dreams are not just frightening or absurd but have something to show us, they will. You do not have to seek dream figures who are giant turtles or dead ancestors. You do not have to dance in a circle, cut your groin, or drink bitter potions. But anticipating a dream may help you evoke the kind of dream you are seeking.

You can give yourself the encouragement you need to dream, give some form to your dream, and let the dream give you some insight into your true feelings about life, just as Native Americans did.

First Dream It—Then Do It

Suppose you were expected to go on a vision quest right there in your hometown. Where would you go? What place would you consider mysterious, sacred, powerful, awe-inspiring, or just downright forbidden? What kind of dream would you be looking for? What kind of guide would you want to show up in your dreamworld? What would this creature look like? Sound like? What kind of questions would you ask of this mystery guide?

What would your protective song sound like? What would be the kind of magical object you would like to keep with you to ward off danger?

Write these things down, draw them, or even say them—whisper them!—into a tape recorder. Just remember them, because later on, they might come in handy.

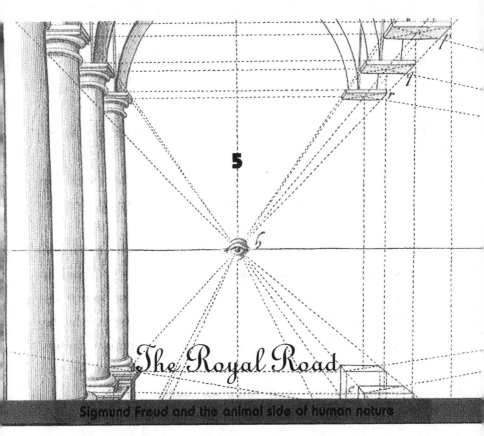

5

The Royal Road

Sigmund Freud and the animal side of human nature

o you know the name Sigmund Freud? Raise your hand if you do. Just as I thought, you have most likely heard of Freud!

Do you know the name but absolutely nothing else about him? Do you associate the name Freud with sex or something that might be uncomfortable to discuss?

Hmmmm . . . probably you do (even if you didn't admit it).

Ask somebody down at your local donut shop who Sigmund

Freud was and you'll probably hear something like "He was the sex doctor, right?"

(OK, don't actually do this, because there's always a chance somebody will think you're making fun of him and fling a cruller at you or something.)

The fact is that Freud is one of those immensely influential thinkers whose name has become a word itself (as in "Freudian symbol" or "Freudian slip") and who is known (and sometimes reviled) by people throughout the world who have no idea what he actually said or meant. Freud is a tremendously controversial figure in modern history—he was controversial in his own day, and he remains a source of scorn and praise today.

Part of this has to do with his own personality. Like many highly intelligent, ambitious men and women, Freud was difficult, proud, quick to take offense, and fiercely defensive about his ideas and theories.

But the ideas and theories themselves are also to blame for some of the attacks he received and still receives. Yes, Freud talked a lot about sex, and that upset people in his own day and still causes lots of people to gnash their teeth when they hear his name.

But much more important, Freud was instrumental in making the modern world look at itself in the mirror. Freud was wrong about some things—perhaps many things—but the one undeniable truth he proclaimed was that the human mind was not the cool, calm, reasonable pinnacle of nature's creation, but a teeming closet filled with wishes, desires, and barely understood impulses hiding behind the closed door of reason.

Freud said that reason—which human beings take such pride in and which we believe separates us from the rest of nature—is only part of the story. He said that the animal side of human nature—the wants and needs, the rage and fear—had to be reckoned with, not ignored.

Of course, there were people before Freud who saw that humans did not always act rationally and believed that some of the illnesses and problems besetting the world were caused by the fact that we are so often blind to the truth about ourselves. Artists and writers have said such things since time began.

But in Freud's day—roughly a hundred years ago—the mainstream culture of Europe and America believed in its heart that human beings represented the highest point of natural law, that civilization was progressing inevitably, that we were in every way more in control of our acts and our destiny than we had been in previous eras, and that reason and science could lead us permanently out of darkness into the light.

This was before the two world wars, of course, and before reason and science helped develop weapons of mass destruction. But Freud saw clearly that society was filled with conflicts, that the rational was forever at war with the irrational, that the urge toward peace and civilization was constantly undermined by fear, anger, and misunderstanding, and that humans were themselves torn between the uplifting and the animal sides of our nature.

And, Freud argued, it is precisely in our dreams that these conflicts emerge to disturb and haunt us—or to be thrust away, out of sight into our unconscious. He called dreams "the royal road to the unconscious," the best route to self-understanding.

"A dream is the fulfillment of a wish."
—Sigmund Freud

We don't have time, really, to consider Freud's rather interesting life story (but you can read more about it—see the appendix). Still, it's impossible to talk about dreams without talking about Freud. In many people's minds, the two are inextricably linked. That makes sense, because Freud's first ascent to fame was through his book *The Interpretation of Dreams* originally published in 1900.

And though lots of people disagree with Freud's conclusions about dreams (and he himself revised and contradicted his own theories for the rest of his life), few people would disagree that

Freud helped make the study of dreams respectable, important, and central to the understanding of the human mind.

Freud's dream theory was rather complicated (and *The Interpretation of Dreams* is hard to plow through!), but some of his ideas can be boiled down like this:

1. *Dreams come from the unconscious and are mostly made up of disguised wishes bubbling to the surface.*

   Freud did not invent the idea of the unconscious, but he was the first to map out this uncharted territory of the mind. Our conscious mind, of course, is what we think with. Freud believed that we possess another mind as well, the unconscious, which he saw as rather like an attic stuffed with ideas, fantasies, wishes, and memories that have never been conscious and with those images and impulses that have been banished to the unconscious because the conscious mind cannot deal with them.

2. *The wishes, fantasies, and images expressed in our dreams often (though not always) deal with sexual desires—especially with what Freud called "the Oedipus Complex" (you've probably heard about this).*

   Oedipus, as you probably know, was the ancient Greek king who killed his father and married his mother. He didn't want to—he even tried to avoid it—but fate had ordained this path for him.

Freud said that this dark fantasy is true for all children: all little boys want to destroy their fathers so they can solely possess the love of their mothers; all little girls want to get rid of their mothers so they can have their fathers to themselves. Freud said this was a natural urge yet one that children cannot cope with and that the urge is repressed into the unconscious where it simmers along, bubbling into our dreams.

3. *Dreams come to us in two separate layers—the manifest content and the latent content.*

Freud believed that there was a function of the brain dedicated to censoring even our dreams, so that the "manifest content" of the dream, what you actually remember, is merely the disguise for the "latent content" of the dream, what the dream actually means. This is where the idea of Freudian symbols comes from.

The part of the dream you recall, Freud argued, is like a code or a puzzle, and it is only in working through the confused symbols that we see the disguised wish behind the dream.

4. *We can understand our dreams only by finding the deeper meaning buried in the superficial memory of the dream.*

Freud said that our memories of dreams often work by "displacement." That means the most important element of the dream is shoved aside by some much less important dream image or activity, because the censoring part of our mind does not wish to consider the darker images of the unconscious. We can reach that displaced element through "free association," letting our thoughts and words spill out in response to a cue from a therapist (or from ourselves).

For instance, one of Freud's patients who was in great personal distress dreamed of being handed a comb by a stranger. She thought the dream was trivial and could not understand why it bothered her so much. In free-associating on the word "comb," she discovered that she connected combing her hair with something she had heard from her parents in childhood about how disgusting it was to allow someone else to use your comb—to mix your hair with theirs, so to speak.

In further work, it turned out that this patient had recently argued with her parents about a marriage proposal from a Christian (she was Jewish) which would form a mixed marriage. Freud asserted that the stranger handing her the comb showed that she really wanted to pursue this relationship, though her parents objected. The comb was the displaced sexual symbol, demonstrating this woman's latent wish.

Though Freud went on to write numerous other works and to theorize on an astonishing range of subjects, his ideas about dream interpretation are probably his most influential. *The Interpretation of Dreams* sold only 351 copies in its first edition, but it eventually went through seven new editions, has been translated into virtually every language on earth, and has never been out of print since its first publication (there are only a handful of books—like the Bible—about which this can be said).

What about this idea that Freud saw everything in sexual terms? Freud himself seemed to be divided about this most famous aspect of his theories. He said, on the one hand, "The assertion that all dreams require a sexual interpretation, against which critics rage so incessantly, occurs nowhere in my *Interpretation of Dreams* . . . and is in obvious contradiction to other views expressed in it."

On the other hand, in the same book, he said, "All elongated objects, such as sticks, tree trunks, and umbrellas . . . may stand for the male organ. Boxes, cases, chests, cupboards, and ovens represent the uterus. Steps, ladders, or staircases, or . . . walking up and down them are representations of the sexual act . . ." I think it's fair to say that Freud was a little obsessed with sexual symbols and perhaps gave them more weight than they deserve. We do see sexual symbols throughout art and history and life; how could we not? Sex is a favorite preoccupation of the human species. But there are other conflicts in our lives and other messages the unconscious may be trying to send our way. There are even wishes other than sexual ones that we cannot acknowledge and that might steam up out of the cauldron of our unconscious.

It was over this issue of sexual symbolism in our dreams and the importance of the sex drive in human nature that Freud did battle with a number of his colleagues and disciples, most famously Carl Jung (next chapter!).

It's also true, as many feminists have pointed out, that Freud was largely clueless about women and considered them merely damaged men. But that was overwhelmingly the view of Freud's era, and it does no good to act as if people in the past ought to have known better. In the future, people will say that of us, too!

So, we must not dismiss Freud because of his imperfections. Most great thinkers are not necessarily nice people, and they may even be fools at times. But Freud truly changed the way the human mind was perceived. He inspired countless scientists and writers and artists and ordinary people to pay attention to dreams and to the whisperings of their inner selves. He blazed a trail through that shadowy land where instincts, memories, wishes, and impulses dance freely—the unconscious.

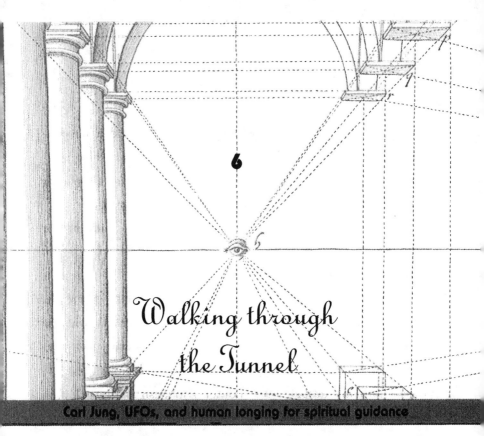

6

Walking through the Tunnel

Suppose you had a very close friend, someone to whom you had confided your deepest beliefs about life, and you began to suspect that this friend wasn't really your friend and was going around telling people that he disagreed with you about the very beliefs you had confided to him.

That's what Sigmund Freud thought about his colleague and disciple Carl Jung.

Suppose you had a friend who was older than you and she constantly treated you like she was your mother or older sister, belittling what you had to say and suggesting you were being a bit foolish because you had ideas with which she disagreed.

That's what Carl Jung thought about his colleague and mentor Sigmund Freud.

They were probably both right.

Freud and Jung were friends and enemies, colleagues and rivals. The two of them helped create a real revolution in the way the human mind is regarded, yet after their intensive seven-year friendship they had a huge falling-out, and to this day their followers cordially despise one another and bash one another in books and journals.

I'm not making this up!

Carl Jung was nineteen years younger than Freud and from a completely different background. While Freud was the son of a Jewish merchant, never entirely at home in the culture of his adopted homeland Austria, Jung was Swiss, the only son of a well-known Protestant minister. Jung grew up surrounded by other family members who were deeply involved in the mainstream religious culture of Europe.

Jung was intrigued by spiritualism and the occult in his youth

and never lost that interest, while Freud was a dedicated material-
ist who believed that the impulse toward religion was a human
error expressing repressed sexuality and guilt.

How on earth did they ever get to be friends?

They were drawn together because of the bold, new path Freud
was blazing in the field of psychoanalysis. Jung showed an early
inclination toward the study of the human mind, and in the early
twentieth century, Freud was *the man*, the one who was shaking up
the establishment and causing astonishment and outrage. It would
be like being drawn to professional basketball in the late 1990s—
you'd want to get to know Dennis Rodman, probably, even if you
didn't think you'd like him.

Freud and Jung quickly discovered that despite their differences
they had a lot in common: a fascination with dreams and a belief
that the messages dreams sent to us were subtle and significant.

When they met in 1907 they talked nonstop for thirteen hours!
Freud was tremendously impressed by Jung and saw in him what
he called his "apostle to the gentiles."

What did he mean by that?

Because Freud and most of his early followers were Jewish,
Freud feared that his new theories of psychoanalysis would be
branded a "Jewish science" by the deeply anti-Semitic culture of

early twentieth-century Europe. For his part, Jung was thrilled to be considered the crown prince of this new movement; he said that Freud was the first man of importance he had ever met.

The disagreements were already present, but both Freud and Jung ignored them, just as we often ignore the nagging voice that tells us that our new friendship or our new romance isn't going to work out.

For one thing, Jung disagreed with Freud's belief that the Oedipus complex was at the heart of all emotional disturbances and that sexuality was central to the development of human experience.

He was also not convinced that free association was the best route to the secrets we lock up inside our unconscious. He suggested that free association led outward, away from the actual image, and that instead we need to focus very deeply and specifically on the picture offered to us by a dream.

In many ways, their philosophical disagreements reflected their personalities. Freud was pessimistic about human beings, perceiving their animal impulses always on the verge of strangling the more noble aspects of the mind. He saw the unconscious as a dark, dangerous jungle that must be crossed in order to reach normality. Jung saw the human spirit as striving toward wholeness, attempting to integrate all sides of its nature. He saw the unconscious as a fascinating underground labyrinth to be traveled through with wonder and visited for inspiration.

In later years, they would both make it seem that they had argued over a wide range of issues. But it was dreams that truly caused their rift.

That's one reason why we're spending some time on this relationship. Imagine feeling so strongly about dreams that you got into a fist fight with your brother or refused to speak again with your best friend! That's what this was like (well, no fist fight, but you get the idea).

In 1909, Freud and Jung sailed to America to lecture on psychoanalysis at Clark University, in Massachusetts. To pass the time on the voyage, Freud and Jung agreed to analyze each other's dreams.

But in one of these dream sessions, Jung asked Freud for some more specific personal details so that he could interpret the dream more easily. Freud balked, saying that he would not divulge any more information. Why? "I cannot risk my authority," Freud said. Jung felt betrayed. He perceived that Freud considered his own authority more important than the truth.

On the same voyage, Jung had an elaborate dream about exploring his house, descending through various ancient rooms he had never been aware of, and discovering a cavelike tomb where there were two skulls.

Freud had difficulty interpreting this dream, and while Jung felt that the ancient rooms had significance to his ideas about the human mind, Freud focused on the two skulls, demanding to know from Jung whose they were and who it was that he wished dead.

Jung realized that Freud needed to interpret the dream as a wish fulfillment dream to bolster his theory that all dreams harbored secret wishes. Jung feared that an argument would erupt if he contradicted Freud, so he told him that the skulls might belong to his wife and sister-in-law. Freud saw this as vindicating his theories. But to Jung, this confirmed his fear that Freud was too narrowly focused, that he refused to consider alternate possibilities to his theories.

Their relationship continued to be strange and full of contradictions. In 1909, Jung visited Freud and they had a heated discussion about Jung's interest in parapsychology (extrasensory perception, the idea that mental energy can cause physical reactions in the world). Freud chided Jung in a condescending way, and instead of responding, Jung repressed his anger. Jung's chest grew hotter and hotter with anger, and suddenly there was a loud bang that came from the bookcase. Jung predicted there

"We may expect to find in dreams everything that has ever been of significance in the life of humanity."

—Carl Jung

would be a second loud noise, and there was a few moments later, bang!

According to Jung, Freud looked as if he had seen a ghost, but later, Freud wrote to Jung saying that this experience did not prove the existence of mind-over-matter but was simply a delusion the two of them had together.

Maybe the bang was just a delusion, but it certainly seemed to point toward the blowup that was to come. In 1912, Jung lectured at a conference at Fordham University, in New York. He went there with the purpose of defending Freud, but the lecture vehemently disagreed with many Freudian ideas. Freud believed Jung had sabotaged him. The next time they met, Freud fainted, and a few months later they exchanged their final letters. They never met, wrote, or spoke again.

But bizarre as this friendship was, Jung's story should not be seen as just a spinoff of the story of Freud. Jung's ideas about dreams were complex and unique. Here are some of them:

1. *Dream images and symbols cannot be boiled down to simple equations.*

   Where Freud would say that walking through a tunnel represented sexual intercourse, Jung would ask, "Who is doing the walking? What does the walker feel like as he proceeds through the tunnel? What is on the other side of the tunnel?" Jung believed that the dreamer's whole life had to be taken into account in order to fully understand the meaning of dream symbols.

2. *Dreams do not necessarily focus on the past. They tell us what is going on in our unconscious here and now.*

   Unlike Freud, who saw dreams largely as a key to unlocking childhood trauma, Jung believed that dreams spoke of the present as well. Dreams are the expression of our unconscious as it tries to integrate the past and present, the male and female, and the dark and the bright side of the human spirit. The struggle for wholeness and for self-understanding, which Jung saw as a *spiritual quest*, plays itself out each night in our dreams.

3. *There is no latent content to dreams. The dream's meaning is there for us to interpret.*

"The manifest dream-picture is the dream itself," Jung argued, "and contains the whole meaning of the dream." The reason dreams seem incomprehensible to us, he suggested, is that we do not speak their language. It is as if a message were being sent to us in an ancient language with which we were only slightly familiar.

So, instead of free association, we need "direct association" or "dream amplification," a way in which we can see what ideas, word, pictures, and beliefs are associated in our thoughts with the obscure images in the dream. Jung would often suggest that a patient describe for him an object in the patient's dream as if to someone who had absolutely no idea what such an object was. In that way, the *context* of the dream symbols might be established.

4. *Dreams often follow a dramatic structure.*

Jung described dreams as a "drama taking place on one's interior stage." He said dreams often behave as if they were classical plays with an opening scene that introduces the characters, setting, and situation of the dream; the development of plot and conflict; the response to the conflict by the main player; and some sort of resolution of the dramatic conflict. This resolution is either within the dream or after the dream has ended and the dreamer awakens with new insight. Often, Jung believed, the final images of a dream pose solutions that the dreamer must consider in solving the problem in real life. These solutions might be metaphorical (not direct answers), but they address a problem introduced at the beginning of the dream.

5. *There are significant dreams and insignificant dreams. There are also grand dreams, which are not merely about ourselves but about human nature itself.*

Jung believed that certain dream images, which he called "archetypes," were not merely coming from our personal memory but from a sort of human racial memory, which he called "the collective unconscious." This is why, he said, the images of the slaying of the beast, the divine child, the shadow or double, the wise old man, and the "mandala," or sacred wheel, appear in art, mythology, and religions throughout the world. They are archetypal dream images, which spoke to our ancestors and continue to speak to us today about the human spirit.

Jung lived much later into the twentieth century than

Freud did and wrote even more widely than Freud. He was fascinated by world religions, by the philosophies of ancient China and India, and even by UFOs. He was the first major thinker to take seriously the idea of what were then called "flying saucers," which he believed were modern projections of human longing for spiritual guidance, like the visions of spirits and demons from previous eras.

Jung was often accused of being a mystic, and there are plenty of people who find his writings a bit thick, really, full of strange words and not entirely understandable ideas. He was, perhaps, more a philosopher than a man of science, yet Jungian psychology has flourished in the past twenty years, and many scholars consider Jung tremendously influential not only in dream theory but in the art and literature of the contemporary world. He was among the first scientists to try linking Western rational thought with Eastern spirituality.

But as with Freud, we don't have to agree with everything he thought and said to see him as a towering figure in the human race's search for self-knowledge. And like Freud, Jung, too, should be hailed as a guiding spirit as we continue our journey through the labyrinth of dreams.

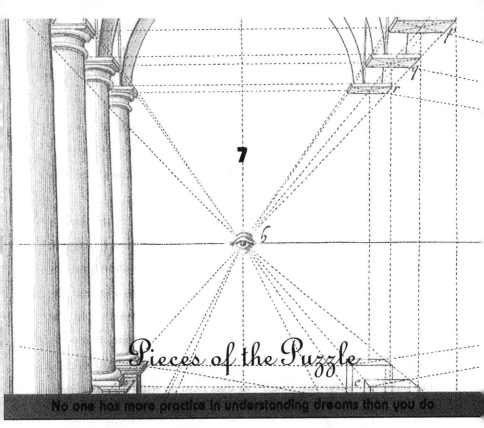

7

Pieces of the Puzzle

We've taken a look at how dreams have been viewed by shamans, priests, and famous psychologists. How do people a bit more like you see their dreams?

A little later in this book, you'll find a dream questionnaire—which I hope you'll fill out—and some of the responses I collected from students and former students and assorted other dream enthusiasts. It was a tool I used in writing this book.

Why should it matter what you or what my students say about their dreams? Why shouldn't it? You have ideas about the mind and experience of someone your age that a world-famous psychologist may well have forgotten.

This sort of grassroots approach is one of the fastest growing areas of dream study. The idea is that while experts may have great insight into the theory of dream analysis, no one has more practice in appreciating or understanding dreams than average dreamers do.

It's a sort of democratic approach to dream interpretation, and it fits in with all kinds of other studies that suggest that what ordinary people have to say about a subject (war, sex, current events) may shed as interesting a light on that field as what a professional historian says.

In other words, you don't have to be Freud or Jung or a priest of Asclepius; you can be Joe or Joann Student and still have something valuable to say about those puzzles and poems from the unconscious. Like these dreamers:

"I am in a swimming pool (large, expansive) and need to get across. I know that my mom is also in the pool. She is wearing the fuzzy blue caftan she wears around the house in the mornings. All I know in the dream is that my focus is on getting to the other side of the pool, and I leave her where she is. It is understood in the dream that she will drown, but I just leave her there. I remember thinking in the dream that I or my character in the dream was afraid to touch the bottom of the pool, because I didn't want my toes to bump into my mother's dead body or any other dead bodies—the dream implied there were more down there.

"What does it mean? Because I swim away from her I obviously do not intend to carry her weight. Is this my dream's way of saying she is an emotional burden in real life? I am growing up and trying to do things for myself and my future, which she is unaccepting toward, so I am definitely trying to cut the thread to that dependent child-mom routine, both in dreams and in real life. And she is very dependent on me. Maybe it's resentment manifested. As I swim away in the dream, I don't give her a second thought until the realization that it's too late to save her. Then, instead of feeling strong horror, I feel dread of bumping into her with my toes, not guilt but fear of the consequences!"

—Martha Balin

"When I was about twelve or thirteen, I had a series of dreams in which I killed my father, always out of some self-defense scenario. This was most definitely a reflection of deep anger (I can't think of a better word than "anger," although that does not encompass it all) toward my father that I have struggled with for years. In college, I had a series of dreams in which the rock singer Melissa Etheridge beat up a number of men in my life. In my dreams, she acted as a representative of me, and I enjoyed every minute of it!"

—Jennifer Cislo

"Once, I woke up from a dream laughing. There was a van with an alien in the back, and some people I knew from school were guarding it and letting it eat only Cup-a-Soups. I bought myself a dreamer's dictionary a couple of years ago. It was fun, but more often than not I would create my own interpretations and feel better about them than the dictionary's. For instance, if I dreamed about a wolf (one of my favorite animals) I would see that as a positive symbol. The dictionary claimed that wolves in a dream were only a good sign if you killed them.

"For the most part, I feel that I can understand dreams on my own. I don't think my dream involving a shark attack necessarily means I'm going to be eaten while swimming that day. It might have to do with people in my life who are shark-like. If the dream makes me feel afraid or uncomfortable I remind myself to watch out for nasty people. I believe that negative dreams are there to keep you on your toes. They wake you up with a warning and usually teach you a lesson if you look closely enough."

—Dakota Shepard

"I once had a dream where I was walking along the sidewalk with a group of the friends I hung around with in sixth grade. A red sports car drove up next to us and a lady I didn't know got out and pulled me away from the group kicking and crying and kidnapped me.

"At the time, I wasn't getting along with those friends so well. Maybe I'd sort of outgrown them. I think the dream was trying to tell me to start moving away from that crowd, to make new friends. Maybe the lady was supposed to be my mother, who didn't really like these friends, or maybe she was part of me, the part that knew it was time to move on."

—Jim Cleary

"I'm in an amusement park, riding on a Ferris wheel. The sounds of children laughing and music playing are in the background. The Ferris wheel is turning, and I'm at the top. All of a sudden, the sky gets dark and the wheel starts moving. I look down at the other seats below me only to find that I am the only one on the ride. I am stranded on top of this Ferris wheel, unable to descend. I begin screaming, but there is no one there to listen to my cry for help. I am alone.

"I had this dream a few weeks before I was going to move away to college. It could depict my departure from a secure home to living on my own. In a dream dictionary I consulted, it said that being high up can depict feeling isolated from the known and secure. I was finally getting my independence, but it was frightening in the beginning. I didn't know what to expect, just like you feel on a ride at an amusement park."

—Melissa Ruggieri

These dreamers are not much older and probably not much more versed in dream lore than you are. They are not experts, but they have all instinctively understood that dreams often speak to us in metaphors. When one dreamer wanted to get back at men she resented in her life, she subconsciously chose to use the image of the well-known lesbian singer Melissa Etheridge; when another dreamer was experiencing anxiety about change in her life, she imagined herself stranded at the top of a giant wheel—something that turns and turns, sort of the way the world does.

Some dreams are harder to interpret, of course, and some even defy understanding. But many dreams unfold to us the way a good story or a poem does—we might not know exactly what the author (our unconscious!) has in mind, but we get the idea, and it intrigues us.

First Dream It—Then Do It

Go somewhere quiet and peaceful or somewhere you feel comfortable, and for three minutes, write, speak, or draw something you remember from a dream. Later on, we'll talk about how best to recall dreams, and we'll take a look at some tips to help understand dreams, too. But for now, your task is to get some of those strange fragments out of your memory and onto paper (or tape or disk).

Even if you rarely remember your dreams, you probably have some piece of a dream that you do recall. It's likely to be a scary or unpleasant one, since those are the ones we tend to remember. But it might just be a silly one, like the alien drinking the Cup-a-Soups. Try to get the feeling of the dream, even if you can't recall all the specifics. Then stop. Think back. What was going on in your life at that moment? Does anything stand out? Do you recall what you were doing the day you had the dream? Any conversation, disagreement, or unpleasant experience you had around that time? Anything you wish you had said or done around then that you didn't do?

Maybe, if you think about it you'll have an idea or a small piece of an idea of what this dream was saying to you. Maybe you won't. But hold onto this! Once you've read a little further, you might find that the pieces of the dream puzzle are actually in your own hands!

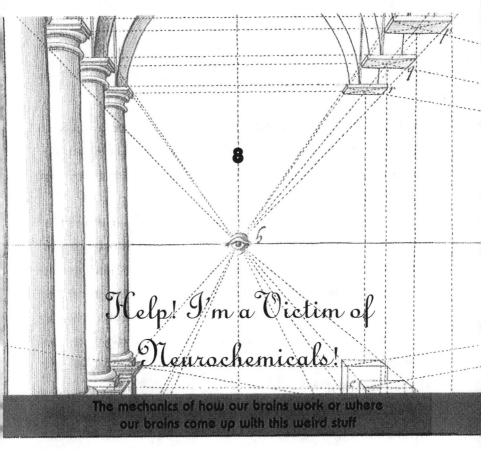

8

Help! I'm a Victim of Neurochemicals!

The mechanics of how our brains work or where our brains come up with this weird stuff

So far, we've talked about dreams in more or less familiar ways: dreams as religious, psychological, creative, or just plain peculiar mental experiences.

But dreams are more (or some people would say less) than that. Dreams are also biological and physiological events occurring in that remarkable, complex, and little understood organ we call the brain.

Dreams may be messages to us from our unconscious, but before they can be messages, they have to happen. They have to be produced and transmitted by the chemicals and electrical impulses coursing through our cerebral cortex.

There are a lot of important and controversial issues involved in the study of what goes on in the brain. Is the human brain just an elaborate (and somewhat squishy) computer? Is the mind—what we call consciousness or self-awareness—distinct from the brain? How is consciousness produced by the brain? Do other animals have consciousness or just instinct? To what extent are our thoughts, feelings, and dreams separate from the billions of cells that produce them?

Well, we won't be answering those questions in this book (just writing them down gives me a headache), but in order to have a better picture of the process of dreaming, we do need to take a glance at what scientists believe happens in our brains while we sleep.

The problem is, of course, that we can't actually see what's going on in the brain; we can only see the physical evidence that the brain produces. Wouldn't it be wonderful to be able to videotape our dreams so we could play them back and learn from them? And wouldn't it be wonderful if we could actually get a small camera inside the brain to take snapshots of all the changes that occur in the brain when we think and when we dream?

But so far, we can't. We can only measure things like electrical activity in the brain and levels of chemical compounds found in brain cells and make inferences based on those measurements.

Modern research into the sleeping brain began in 1953, when the American physiologist Nathaniel Kleitman noticed that the sleeping infants he was studying seemed to have distinct periods of sleep during which their eyes moved wildly behind closed eyelids.

Kleitman found that sleeping adults displayed this rapid eye movement (REM) as well, and when he used an electroencephalograph (EEG)—a machine that maps out the brain's electrical activity—he found that the periods of REM sleep were always accompanied by certain kinds of brain waves. When adults were awakened from these REM sleep periods, they nearly always reported that they had been dreaming.

Kleitman and his colleagues believed they had discovered the key to dreaming, and it was widely assumed for many years that all dreaming took place during REM sleep. This turns out not to be true—we dream throughout the night—but REM dreaming is usually richer, more visual, and more storylike than dreams that occur in other periods of sleep.

Reports about non-REM dreams seem to show that they are more like snapshots or drifting thoughts. REM dreams are the dreams you are probably thinking of when you wake up and murmur, "What a weird dream!"

Further study of brain waves has shown that our sleep cycles are made up of four separate stages.

Stage 1, which lasts about ten minutes, is a transitional stage, and the brain behaves more or less as if it were still awake. Stages 2 and 3, which last between twenty and forty-five minutes each, are increasingly deeper sleep. Stage 4 is the stage where your brain is functioning altogether differently from the way it does when you are awake.

Following stage 4, which can last as long as an hour, you return to stage 2, and then you enter REM sleep, usually for about ten minutes. That's one complete cycle. Then, the cycle starts all over again (without stage 1, the falling-asleep stage), but in each successive cycle, REM sleep is longer and longer. Depending on the individual and the amount of time you sleep, you might have four different sleep cycles during the night. By morning, REM sleep can last as long as an hour.

Does that sound complicated? There's more!

Throughout these sleep cycles, our brains are abuzz with

activity, just as they are while we are awake. But as we are falling asleep, a set of neurochemicals, which originate in the brain stem, begin shutting off certain brain functions and simultaneously turn up the volume, so to speak, on other functions.

The neurochemicals norepinephrine and serotonin, which are most active during the waking state, are shut off during REM sleep. These chemicals are involved in regulating pain, taste, and smell. This may explain why we do not experience pain when the blue dinosaur grabs our legs and why the sensory experiences of tasting and smelling—so important in our waking lives—are rarely involved in our dreams.

"What did I dream I do not know

The fragments fly like chaff

Yet, strange, my mind was tickled so

I cannot help but laugh."

—Robert Graves

These same neurochemicals may also control the reality-testing function of our brains, so that our dreaming minds are not surprised when we fly through the air or when our friends turn into wolves.

But wait! There's more!

Another neurochemical, acetylcholine, which is not very active while we are awake, suddenly begins sending wave after wave of signals to the brain.

First, these signals stimulate the motor centers of our bodies, which would ordinarily make us run, throw a punch, or leap out of harm's way. But these chemicals are sneaky and also send a signal to the spinal cord saying "Chill!" which causes our muscles to be almost completely paralyzed, except for our eyes.

According to J. Allan Hobson, a renowned psychiatrist and dream researcher at Harvard University, this may explain why our dreams are so often filled with motion—the neurochemicals are ordering our bodies to move while at the same time demanding that they lie still. The only place the chemical demands can be met is in our dreams.

The brain waves that these chemicals create also bombard the emotional circuits of the brain, which may be why so many of our memorable dreams are filled with emotions like anxiety, fear, joy, and anger. These waves even wash through the area of the brain responsible for processing information—and then things really go haywire.

The brain is used to processing external information—what we see and hear and what we make of the world outside. But during this neurochemical free-for-all, all of the sensory input is generated internally by the brain itself, memory, association, and random connections.

That's how dreams are produced, Hobson believes. The higher networks of our brain frantically work to weave stories out of the barrage of sensory input and information they receive from the neurochemicals dancing through them.

Dreams, in other words, may be the tales our higher brains invent to make sense of the bombardment of chemical messages they are receiving from the lower brain.

Hobson calls his theories about the origin of dreams the "activation-synthesis model": acetylcholine activates different areas of the brain, and the higher mental centers synthesize the resulting mishmash of information into something resembling a coherent message. The dreams we recall as incoherent, Hobson suggests, are simply a bunch of signals too messy for our brains to organize.

It's important to point out here that this theory is only a theory and it's rather controversial. A lot of dream researchers are intrigued by these ideas, but many feel that Hobson's theory reduces the complexity of dreams—the poetry of the unconscious—to a mechanical model—the random firing of electrons.

"And what is the point of our brains' behaving this way?" others ask. The synthesis-activation model does not seem to offer a completely persuasive answer to that question.

Some experts point out that this whole idea of brain waves and chemicals only applies to REM sleep and can't be considered a complete theory about dreams, since dreaming occurs at other times in the night as well. Others observe that since most people have had, at some point in their lives, a dream they considered to be meaningful and insightful, the activation-synthesis model is ultimately unsatisfying.

If dreams are essentially the product of feverishly overworked brain centers trying to concoct a coherent story out of the nonsense bombarding them, why do we sometimes wake up and say, "Wow! That's really how I feel about her!"?

Hobson himself says he's been misunderstood. He says that the brain has evolved so that it is "inexorably bent upon the quest for meaning." The brain takes the strange and random associations it receives and makes them make sense.

How the brain narrates the story of the dream, turns the chaos into order, and presents the images to us, Hobson says, is not nonsense but rather reveals the dreamer's drives, fears, and associations.

Whew! I'm ready to sleep right now, just worrying about all those chemicals racing around giving off messages.

But just as we aren't going to be able to determine whether dreams hide their real meaning from us, as Freud argued, or whether there is a part of our minds that is filled with images from a collective unconscious, as Jung believed, we aren't going to be able to decide here whether this model of the brain is accurate and, if it is, whether that means dreams are just chemical craziness or harbor some deeper significance. Both ideas may be correct. Gordon Globus, a professor of psychiatry and philosophy at the University of California at Irvine has said, "The findings from sleep research are highly interesting in their way and even necessary. But they tell us almost nothing about what they are supposed to represent. Not one of them brings us a single step nearer to an explanation of dreaming as a unique mode of human existence."

It's a little like the search for the physical origin of the universe. If we discover that there was a giant explosion millions of years ago that created matter as we know it, that doesn't exactly explain why it happened.

If we say that dreams are caused by chemicals, that doesn't entirely explain why they so often feel as if they came out of some shadowy inner chamber of our souls.

The exciting new studies of the human brain may already be turning up new information by the time you read this, and certainly they will give us insights into our dreamworld. But they probably won't give us the ultimate answer. What is the importance of dreaming? What is the meaning of dreaming?

Perhaps an alternate question might be "What is the purpose of being awake? Why are we conscious at all?"

Dreaming and waking are two sides of the same coin, and maybe they can't be—don't want to be—separated.

What do you think?

I'm not going to suggest a project for you here (you probably need a good rest anyway), but if you are intrigued by the whole issue of brain research and neurochemicals (and if you are, shouldn't you alert your physician?), you might want to flip ahead to the reading list in the appendix and see about other books you can read to learn more about it.

That's what the reading list is for!

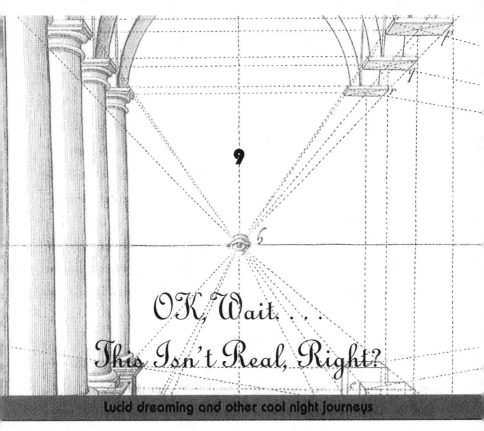

OK, Wait . . . This Isn't Real, Right?

Lucid dreaming and other cool night journeys

Have you ever had a dream in which you asked yourself "Am I dreaming?"

Have you ever been moving through a dream landscape that seemed more or less like real life and then happened upon something—a gigantic red clock, a tree with blue leaves, a person from your real life whose appearance looked off in some way—and stopped within this dream landscape and murmured, "OK, wait, this isn't real, right? This is a dream?"

I'm guessing that you have had experiences like this in your dream life. They're not uncommon. They're called "lucid dreams."

Actually, the examples I've given here would probably be classified as "prelucid" by dream specialists. These kinds of dream experiences are more common than fully lucid dreams.

A lucid dream, in other words, is a dream in which the dreamer becomes aware that he or she is dreaming and may even take some kind of control of the dream state, altering the story of the dream or at least some details within the dream.

Why would anyone want to do such a thing?

There are several reasons. First, it's an exciting discovery to realize that you can exert some kind of power over the often chaotic and bewildering jungle of your dreams. It can make you feel more in control of other aspects of your life, and sometimes it can offer insights into the kinds of obstacles and dilemmas you are encountering in your life and how to deal with them.

And it's a creative act, too. People who become adept at lucid dreaming report that they can travel to paradisical islands, converse with long-lost friends, or invent experiences for themselves they've always wanted to have. Like this dreamer:

"When I become conscious I'm dreaming, I can specifically will a wall to move or an ocean to part. The first time I was ever conscious in my dreams, I willed myself to fly. It was like swimming through the air rather than flying. I saw the details of my hometown and other towns, and they all looked so far away!"

—Glenn Williams

To be conscious while you're dreaming seems like a paradox, doesn't it? Yet, we are certainly aware that it's possible to daydream while we are awake—to be so immersed in a fantasy that we forget where we are and what we are doing. So, why should we not be able to be awake in our dreams?

Although the term "lucid dreaming" was coined by a Dutch psychiatrist in 1913, the concept that we might be conscious while we dream is thousands of years old. The ancient Greek philosopher Aristotle and the early Christian theologian St. Augustine refer to the idea of self-awareness during dreams in their writings.

A nineteenth-century French scholar named Hervey de Saint-Denys was probably the first man to experiment at length with lucid dreaming—or at least, the first man to keep a record of it. Saint-Denys kept a journal of his dreams amounting to 1,946 nights' worth of weirdness. On the 207th night, he suddenly discovered that he could direct the outcome of his dream.

He became so fascinated by this idea that he willed himself to begin lucid dreaming more frequently and eventually claimed to be able to control his dreams at some stage of sleep every night.

In his journals, he gives several examples of his lucid dreams. He conjured up beautiful harem girls (don't tell your folks about this one) and made a frightening monster that was chasing him slow down and then change into a bundle of rags.

The British writer Oliver Fox, who discovered lucid dreaming when he was sixteen, called them "dreams of knowledge," declaring the world of lucid dreaming more vivid and beautiful than any place he had ever experienced in the real world. Even more important than its beauty, Fox said, was the sense of freedom and security he experienced in his lucid dreams, knowing that if danger appeared, he could simply change the dream or wake up.

This is the quality that many dreamers—and many psychologists—have found especially intriguing. Sure, it might be fun to conjure up a bunch of beautiful slaves to do our bidding, but to free ourselves from monsters or to alter a frightening experience might be even more compelling.

"For years, I've had recurring dreams where I'm chased by monsters. Usually I can't see them, but I feel them getting closer and closer. I feel like I'm going to die. A lot of times, the dreams take place in water, and water has always been very frightening to me. Recently, I had a long conversation with a friend who suggested I try lucid dreaming to change the scary direction in which my dreams so often seem to be heading. So, I decided to see if I could be conscious in my dream. I dreamed I was in this huge, dark pool of water. It was like a tunnel, only with water, and there was a monster splashing very close behind me. I ran through the water and I saw a door in the pool or the tunnel or whatever it was. The door looked out of place but I thought 'Wait! I'm dreaming.' So I decided to try and alter the dream.

"I said to myself 'Behind that door is something wonderful and silly, something that will make the monster go away.' I opened the door, and the room was filled with soap bubbles. They came floating out of the room, hundreds of them, and they covered the whole pool of water. Suddenly the monster floated away on the soap bubbles, and I laughed in the dream!"

—Maria Petagna

To prove that lucid dreaming is not just a wacky idea invented by people with hyperactive imaginations, psychologists have performed laboratory studies with striking results.

Dr. Stephen LaBerge, director of the Stanford University Sleep Laboratory, had been experiencing lucid dreams since he was a child and wanted to demonstrate their existence to skeptical colleagues. He agreed to be hooked up to an EEG while he slept and determined that if he did become conscious within his dreams, he would move his eyes from left to right a certain number of times-a movement completely unlike the rapid fluttering of the eyes during REM sleep—to prove that he was in control.

Sure enough, the EEG recorded not only that he was fully asleep during REM, but that his eyes had moved in the predetermined way. He was awakened, and he described the lucid dream he had been having.

LaBerge later developed even more elaborate techniques for reporting lucid dreams. By clenching and unclenching his fist, he was able to communicate in Morse code to laboratory observers while he was still asleep!

He has also invented a somewhat bizarre mechanical device called a Dreamlight. This is a mask that detects eye movements using infrared light and a tiny computer. When the computer counts enough eye movements to classify the sleep stage as REM, little red lights flash within the mask to alert the sleeper that he is dreaming. With these signals, a dreamer can become conscious within his dream and practice lucid dreaming techniques to alter the dream landscape.

Weird, huh? The world of dream studies is a bit like the dream-world itself—serious and absurd at the same time.

But there are less elaborate ways to induce lucid dreaming. In one of his controversial books from the 1960s, anthropologist Carlos Casteneda claimed that an Indian wizard had taught him to gain power over his dreams by looking at his hands within the dream. He trained himself to ask whether or not he was dreaming whenever he looked at his hands within a dream.

A young psychologist named Gary Rogers decided to follow up on this peculiar suggestion. He set the beeper on his watch to go off every ninety minutes, and whenever it went off, he would look at his hands for a few minutes and ask himself if he was awake or dreaming at the time.

After a few days of this, Rogers found that he had conditioned the response so that every ninety minutes—even while in a sleep state—he would look at his hands and wonder if he was dreaming. Eventually, this enabled him to have a lucid dream. While looking at his hands in an REM dream state, he realized that his hands looked different and that he was in fact dreaming.

Other dreamers report similar attempts:

> "In order to become conscious I'm dreaming, I first have to notice some peculiarity in the dreamworld or something that separates it from waking reality. In order to do this, I am always asking myself if I am awake or dreaming. As I sit here typing, I say to myself, 'Am I dreaming?' I answer 'No!' because things are too certain. When I look at my digital clock, it reads 9:53. I look back; it still reads 9:53. OK, I'm not dreaming. If I were, reality would be more fluid; the clock digits might not even be real numbers."
> —Glenn Williams

There is also a technique that Stephen LaBerge developed called Mnemonic Induction of Lucid Dreams (MILD). Using the MILD technique, you wake yourself up from a dream, and then while you are semiawake, you visualize yourself back in that dream and becoming lucid in that dream. You repeat to yourself, "Next time I'm dreaming, I want to recognize I'm dreaming." With practice, this technique may allow you to gradually develop the gift of dream lucidity.

For LaBerge and other psychologists, lucid dreaming is not only a fascinating experience but one with great therapeutic value. If we can place ourselves in what we would consider a terrifying situation and recognize that we are not in danger and that we are not powerless, couldn't that help us make a breakthrough in waking life, too?

Many therapists think so. Some suggest lucid dreaming for their clients who have irrational fears, or "phobias." One man overcame his fear of heights by willing himself to climb higher and higher within a dream; a woman with a lifelong fear of insects willed herself to have a lucid dream in which she shrank to the size of a cockroach and had a conversation with it (OK, maybe that's going too far!).

Other dream researchers suggest that lucid dreaming can be used to converse with and ask advice of long-dead relatives or of someone you've never met whom you respect and would like to have as part of your life, sort of like the spirit guides we talked about back in Chapter 4.

One dream researcher reported that a woman had conversed with Mr. Spock from *Star Trek* in her dreams and that he had helped to guide her out of a dilemma!

But we must remember, also, that lucid dreaming has its limits. It's difficult to accomplish in the first place, and it's even more difficult to retain control of the dream.

Dr. Robert Van de Castle, a renowned dream scholar and author of *Our Dreaming Mind* cautions that we must not expect to be able to alter the entire universe of the dream. You can't necessarily make it stop raining in your dream, for example, but you can alter how you respond to the rain.

Similarly, you can't expect that overcoming a monster in your dreams will make all of your troubles go away; instead, you must try to make your success within the dream a metaphor for your ability to be successful in waking life.

First Dream It—Then Do It

OK, you guessed it. Your next task is to see if you can induce a lucid dream. Don't get discouraged if you can't! It takes time and practice to become skillful at this elusive ability.

You might want to start by reading more about it. Check the reading list in the appendix! Then try this technique called auto-suggestion.

1. Repeat to yourself before you go to sleep, "I will have a lucid dream tonight!" Write it down in a journal or on a word processor, speak it into a tape recorder, or say it over the phone to your best friend (who is liable to say "Huh?" or suggest you see your doctor).

2. Try the hands technique. For several days, set yourself the task of staring at your hands every couple of hours and wondering if you are awake or asleep (don't let too many people see you doing this, though; I don't want to hear that you've been hauled off to a clinic). You have to be thorough about

it! You can't just do it a few times. You have to set yourself a number (say seven times during the day) and a time interval ("I will look at my hands every three hours!") and stick to it.

3. Try to preplan an object or an image that will help you question if you're dreaming or not, if not your hands, then a door, a tree, or a baby carriage. Even if you casually amuse yourself by asking yourself while you're awake if these objects are real or not, you may find they help "cue" lucidity while you're dreaming.

4. If you wake up in the middle of the night, try LaBerge's MILD technique. Visualize yourself back in the dream, visualize yourself becoming lucid, repeat to yourself, "Next time I dream, I want to realize that I'm dreaming."

5. Keep a journal of your efforts (more about this later). And don't give up!

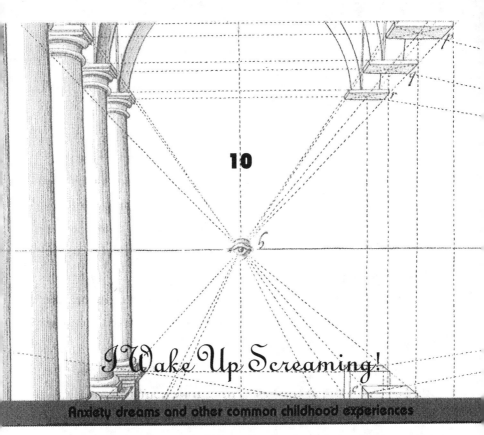

10

I Wake Up Screaming!

Anxiety dreams and other common childhood experiences

When I was a child (about a hundred years ago), I had a series of frightening dreams that I still recall.

I am in the back seat of a large green car. Sometimes my older sister is with me; sometimes she isn't. We are racing down the highway, and it seems to me we are going awfully fast. I look over at the driver's seat to see why my normally cautious father is driving so fast—only he isn't there! No one is driving the car as it hurtles toward a cliff, and I am going over the cliff, falling, falling . . . and I wake up screaming.

Sound familiar?

This is a very common type of childhood nightmare—an anxiety dream in which the dreamer feels helpless to save himself from some terrible fate. It probably stems from our earliest childhood fears. Who's driving this car, anyway? What kind of control can we exert over our lives? Is someone there to help us? Are we all by ourselves?

Going over a cliff in an out-of-control car is one common way of dreaming this problem; being chased by monsters (or some kind of ominous being) is another.

It would be surprising if you had never had a nightmare like this; most of us do, in childhood, though we don't always remember them. We tend to remember them only if they've recurred or if they were especially frightening. (If you don't think you ever had such a dream, you might ask your mother or father if they remember you awakening in the middle of the night, calling out for them. They're much more likely to recall those tiny screams of terror than you are!)

But just as the whole world of dreaming is richer and more complex than we might first imagine it to be, nightmares, too, are more than just scary dreams that can wake you up screaming when you're a kid.

Nightmares occur at all stages of life. Children between the ages of three and six are especially prone to having them and probably have more trouble coping with nightmares than ado-

> *"With Dreams upon my bed thou scarest and affrightest me with Visions."*
> —*William Blake*

lescents and adults do, since the boundaries between what they see at night and what they see during the day are less well defined.

But nightmares are not just for children! They often recur when we are between the ages thirteen and eighteen, brought on, maybe, by the wonderful new varieties of emotional and physical stress of adolescence (but hey, why am I telling *you* about this?).

Stressful life events, illness, and emotional traumas have been shown to produce nightmares in adults, as well. According to Dr. Ernest Hartmann, director of a famous sleep research center in Boston, about 50 percent of the adult population experiences one or two nightmares a year. About 10 percent of the population reports having nightmares once a month or more. Both men and women have nightmares, but men are less likely to want to talk about them (does this surprise you?).

The word "nightmare" actually has nothing to do with a female horse. "Mare" comes from an Old English word that's similar to an Old High German phrase, "mara incubus." An incubus is a demon that comes in the night. For hundreds of years, the expression has referred to any frightening sleep experience—a monster, a demon, the fear these beings produce, or the dream itself.

Dream specialists now say that not all these experiences are the same. There are at least three different kinds of dreams that can wake you up screaming:

1. *Night Terrors.*

These aren't really dreams in the traditional sense but abrupt awakenings, usually early in the sleep cycle, accompanied by sweating, body movements, and often a scream for help. Night terrors are fairly common in children and may even continue into sleepwalking experiences.

When sleep researchers studied night terrors, they discovered that the dreamers' pulse and respiratory rates actually doubled during the terrifying moments of awakening!

Usually, someone who awakens from night terrors will not have a clear memory of a dream, just a sense of utter fear and powerlessness or a feeling of being suffocated or devoured.

"Since I was very young, I've had this recurring dream experience once or twice a year. It's just this utter darkness that is so heavy and suffocating, pushing down on my chest to squeeze out my last breath. I try so hard to wake up from this. I have to fight like hell, because I'm paralyzed. I usually wake up sweating, my muscles and joints aching!"

—Y. Lee

Dream researchers now believe that these night terrors are not REM dreams, but may be what is called a "disorder of arousal." In other words, in people who suffer from night terrors, the brain may have a minor mechanical problem, a difficulty distinguishing between awakeness and sleep. The brain does not properly signal the body to wake up, so the feeling of being choked, suffocated, or unable to arise is registered.

So far, no real cure for night terrors has been found, but most people outgrow them. Sometimes, the night terrors seem to be associated with other physical problems. In one study, children whose adenoids were removed ceased having night terrors.

Night terrors are also terrible for those who observe the dreamers in such a horrifying state:

> "For five minutes I sit up in bed and start to scream as loud as I can. My eyes are open and I look awake, but I'm not. My parents have taken to sleeping as far away from my room as possible, and once an old friend refused to talk to me again when it happened at a friend's house where we'd fallen asleep in the same room. My night terrors have lessened in frequency over the past two years; I wish they'd stop already! I'm afraid to sleep in the homes of people who don't know me well!"
>
> —Michael Housepian

2. *REM Anxiety Dreams.*

These classic nightmares usually occur late in the sleep cycle, during the last three hours of sleep, and are described as long, vivid, often bizarre dreams that awaken the dreamer, who may well respond, "Thank God, that was only a dream!"

These are the scary dreams that seem to touch upon our earliest and most essential fears and may recycle the same kinds of frightening imagery down through the years: being chased by monsters, plummeting through the air in a car or plane, death or dismemberment of ourselves or those we love, or knowing that someone we love is in danger and we can do nothing about it.

Death or the fear of it is a common recurring refrain in these kinds of scary dreams—an obvious allusion to that most basic, universal anxiety, "Am I going to die now?"

"When I was thirteen, I dreamed that a werewolf monster was chasing me all through my house and I was screaming and yelling. My family was able to beat it back with furniture and baseball bats and drive it out of my house onto the basketball court in my front yard (I don't have a basketball court in my front yard). Then the scenery changed and I was back in my house and my family was celebrating the fact that they'd gotten rid of the monster. So I opened my front door, and the monster was waiting for me and it grabbed me. Everyone was celebrating and they didn't hear my screams. The dream was so real that when I woke up, I was actually afraid to open the door to my bedroom in fear of the werewolf monster."

—Khristian Kemp-DeLisser

"I've had a few different versions of this nightmare where my boyfriend has killed someone. I don't know who or why but I know he's going to prison if he gets caught. I wake up from this dream believing that it's happened—and that I'm too late to stop him."

—Dakota Shepard

"As a child I had a nightmare where my father came and slit my mother's, my brother's, and my throats! It scared me to death! I think it had something to do with my fear that my father was too controlling."

—Jessica Tomb

"I dreamed I saw my mother get killed by a huge thing hanging from the top of a gymnasium. It was really big and I lifted it off of her and all I remember was her face was all mutilated and her eyes were hanging out. I cried and cried when I woke up, because it was so disturbing!"

—Kelsey Guntharp

"When I was fourteen, shortly after my parents' divorce, I had a series of bad dreams every single night for almost two weeks. In these dreams, somebody I loved died, in a very realistic way—no monsters, but car wrecks, disease, etcetera. In the second-to-last dream, my father died; the next night I dreamed my mother died, and I woke up literally breathing heavily. That was the last nightmare I had."

—Dodd Bates

There are some ways to treat and even overcome these kinds of frightening dream images. We're going to look at them at the end of this chapter.

3. *Post-Traumatic Stress Nightmares.*

These terrifying dreams are not completely distinct from the last batch, but they have some different qualities. They tend to be recurring, always more or less the same, and always following the same pattern. They tend, also, to be more realistic, replaying images of a terrible event that actually occurred in the dreamer's life. Though the event may be altered or even somewhat disguised, the dreamer almost always knows the experience to which the nightmare is referring.

Men and women who have lived through war or a natural disaster often experience nightly replays of their traumas—running from a tornado or watching their buddies get shot in battle. But sometimes the cause of these traumatic dreams is a different kind of battle or natural disaster, as it was for this dreamer:

"From the age of seven to eleven, I experienced nightmares with a recurring theme or pattern, a variation of the same scenario. The dreams began with a strange man clad in black chasing me, often carrying a weapon. As I ran in fear, I would see my mother in the distance. A wave of security would wash over me, and thus the man in black would disappear. My mother would hover above the creaky stairwell like a ghostly apparition. The white or pink nightgown she wore would float up behind her.

"I raced up the stairs, attempting to grab her hands that were outstretched toward me. She would gaze lovingly into my eyes, and then her expression would change to an evil smile as she let go of my hand. Watching me plummet down the staircase, she laughed and laughed.

"The nightmares coincided with my mother's remarriage to a heartless, sinister man who took pleasure in dominating her and controlling me. He was the bane of my existence, and I blamed my mother. I felt abandoned by the only parent I had ever known.

"The evil in my dreams was inspired by the evil in my life. My mother did not stop the hell; she turned her head and pretended not to see. I believed she no longer cared for me, for she did not protect me from his cruelty and abuse.

"After a stretch of four years, these nightmares ended abruptly after my stepfather's sudden death."

—Jessica Daponte

Sometimes, as in Jessica's case, nightmares cease once the anxiety-producing experience goes away. But, of course, such experiences don't always go away, and some people seem more prone to continued nightmares than others do.

Nightmare expert Dr. Ernest Hartmann suggests that men and women with "thin boundaries"—sensitive, emotional, and creative yet prone to depression—may be more susceptible to these terrors of the night.

Can nightmare sufferers be "cured"?

Hartmann points out that many such people don't want to be cured. They may feel instead that their frightening dreams reveal something unusual about themselves and provide grist for their creative mill.

But for nightmare sufferers who do want to be rid of these pesky demons, one intriguing new approach is to utilize—yes, you guessed it!—lucid dreaming techniques. (If you skipped Chapter 9, go on and flip back to it now; there won't be a quiz.)

Just as Saint-Denys made the monster turn to rags and just as Maria made her monster float away on bubbles, a systematic use of lucid dreaming can allow the nightmare sufferer to rewrite the script of the nightmare, to confront the monster, or even to call upon a "dream friend," a helpful guide whom we imagine or invoke from our real lives to help combat the hideous experience.

In some cases, actually rehearsing a different ending to repetitive nightmares has helped. In other cases, using creative expression—painting, writing, dancing, or acting out the nightmare—has given dreamers insight into their fears and new images to replace the ones that have terrified them.

In one study, a woman who suffered from four nightmares a week underwent therapy that focused on dream-lucidity treatment. After four weekly sessions, her nightmares became less frequent and less vivid. During the seventh week, she dreamed that she was walking up huge gray stairs to a castle; this was a rare good dream, and she felt happy.

In the woman's dream, the stairs went over a moat, and she looked down into the water, where she saw a vicious shark with enormous sharp teeth, which leaped onto the stairs toward her. She was frozen with fear. Then, she realized that she had been having a good dream until the shark appeared—lucidity! She stared at the shark, much as Saint-Denys had stared at his monster. The shark turned into a huge, smiling whale, and she awoke feeling fine.

By facing the fear, she overcame it—in fact, she befriended it! This, in turn, allowed her to face some of her emotional difficulties in waking life, too.

Take that, monsters!

OK, here's another peculiar project. It has four possible parts.

1. Try to remember a childhood nightmare. Try to write it down, record it, or draw it. Consider especially what it looked like. What color monster chased you? What kind of hideous creature threatened you? Who else was in the nightmare with you? Where did it take place? Do any of the nightmares mentioned here relate to your nightmare?

2. Do an informal survey of your family members and friends. Do any of them recall nightmares from when they were younger? Try to get as many people as you can to describe their nightmares to you. Of course, some people won't want to, but you'll probably be surprised how many people recall a scary dream from their childhood and how many people actually enjoy recalling them—after all, the fear is probably far away by now.

3. If any of your friends or family members are interested, you might have an informal nightmare session, where you read the nightmares aloud, draw them, or try to act them out. This is like a dream group, which we'll talk more about in Chapter 19, only with nightmares.

4. If you or your friends sometimes still have nightmares, you might want to try the rewriting-the-script approach. Try imagining—by yourself or in a group—what some silly, funny, harmless ending might be to the horrible dream scenarios you sometimes experience. How could a plummeting car be saved in your dreams? How could the werewolf be vanquished, confronted, or banished? How could you stop your sister from being torn to pieces?

This isn't just for entertainment—though it should be entertaining! Comparing your monsters with the monsters of your friends and siblings will probably show you how similar are the fears we all have, how horrifyingly creative our unconscious can be, and how it is possible to gain some control even over these most terrifying visitors of the night.

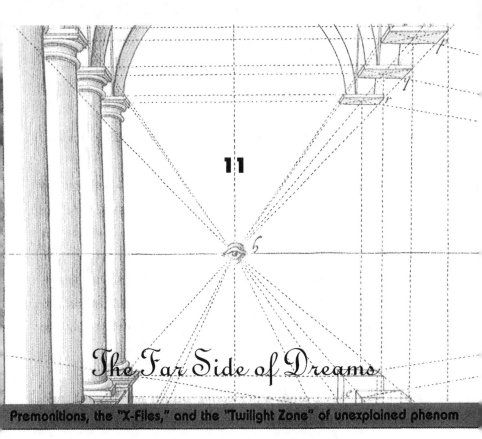

11

The Far Side of Dreams

*I*n 1966, a Welsh girl named Eryl Mai Jones woke up one morning and wanted badly to tell her mother about an ominous dream she had just had. Eryl Mai often wanted to discuss her dreams with her mother, but her mother, like mothers everywhere, was too busy or just not interested in her daughter's peculiar night visions.

But that morning, the mother listened as Eryl Mai described her dream. She and her friends had gone to school, Eryl Mai told her mother, but the school was gone, buried under something huge and black. She concluded her strange tale by saying, "I'm not afraid to die, Mommy. I'll be with Peter and June."

Two days later, a coal slide engulfed Eryl Mai's hometown; 144 people died. Eryl Mai, Peter, and June were among the 118 school children who were buried alive when their school was crushed by the coal.

OK, that's pretty creepy, but it really happened. An English psychiatrist did a study about this disaster and found at least twenty-five other credible accounts of dreams that seemed to predict this disaster in the Welsh coal mining town of Aberfan.

Does that seem to defy logic and probability? Just wait.

In 1902, J. W. Dunne, a pioneering British aeronautical engineer, dreamed of a volcanic eruption on the island of Martinique, a place he had never been or even thought about. In the dream, Dunne tried to warn French authorities, telling them that Mt. Pelée would erupt, killing four thousand people. A few days later, he saw a newspaper headline. Mt. Pelée had erupted, killing not four thousand but forty thousand people.

OK, that's even creepier. Dunne's dream appears to have foreseen a natural disaster that had nothing to do with him—and the dream only got one zero wrong in the prediction of fatalities.

Dunne himself was so distressed by the experience that he

devoted much of his time and energy to researching spooky dreams like his and devising an elaborate theory of time to explain how it is possible to see the future in our dreams. He believed that human beings are like a man rowing a boat up a river—the man can see where he has been but not where he is going. In his book *An Experiment with Time* Dunne suggests that in the dream state, we are freed from this constraint, able to see the whole river of time.

Not entirely convincing?

These two dramatic examples represent what we call "the far side of dreaming," dreams that seem to push beyond the merely ordinary weirdness we have already considered into some peculiar twilight zone, where probability and logic falter, where explanations are not entirely convincing.

Probably, you've never had a catastrophe dream that came true (or I would surely have seen your story on *Unsolved Mysteries*), but you might have had a lesser version of some of these far side dreams—a premonition dream or a more specific precognitive dream, maybe even a shared dream. So, let's cruise through this creepy cul-de-sac of the dream landscape before we lose our nerve.

A "premonition" is a feeling that something is about to happen, usually to ourselves or someone we know and love. It's like a hunch, only a bit more specific. In a dream premonition, you wake up with this feeling, which can range from the more or less trivial (a dream that you're going to have a quiz in math) to the downright eerie (a dream about your friend's illness).

But though they are peculiar and unsettling to us, a lot of these tremors from the far side can be explained without delving too deeply into the "X-Files."

For instance, years ago, a friend of mine awoke from a dream in which she saw her boyfriend total his car and badly injure himself in a highway accident. A few days later, he did just that. She was understandably shaken up by this experience and still doesn't like to talk about it. She is convinced that she had a psychic experience, and maybe she did. But that boyfriend had a drinking problem and lived fifty miles away; he often drove to see her after he'd already had too many drinks, and they had argued about it not long before she had that dream.

If your boyfriend drives drunk a lot, it's not too great a stretch of the imagination to think that your unconscious might issue you a warning: this guy is trouble. The most powerful tool of the unconscious is a dream. The dream did predict the accident, but it may have been more a case of my friend's unconsciously putting two and two together than of literally seeing the future.

Many premonitions have this quality. Psychologists call it "fine cueing." Your unconscious picks up on a nonverbal warning from your teacher that there will be a quiz or senses that a friend is depressed and may try to harm herself even though your conscious mind blocks out the teacher's cue or the fear that your friend might need your help.

But there are more complex versions of these dream warnings, too, warnings that cannot be so easily rationalized. A "precognitive dream," like a premonition, seems to offer us knowledge of something that is about to happen. But these dreams are often more detailed—and the details may prove to be eerily true.

"I dreamed that I was in a hospital intensive care unit. In the hospital bed there was a person basically mutilated and disfigured from surgery. As I turned to leave, the nurse stopped me and asked me if I wanted a job in the ICU. I said 'No,' that I already had other jobs. She asked me for my phone number, and I could see that as she wrote it down, she wrote the word 'friend' instead of my name. I repeated again that I did not want the job, that I could not handle it, pointing at the person who was in the bed, who was terribly disturbing to me. The nurse said 'You already have the job.' I couldn't stop talking to people about this dream, I was so disturbed by it. Several weeks after the dream, one of my closest friends called to tell me that her cancer had recurred after two years of remission. Within a week, she was lying in intensive care after surgery and I was sitting by her side. I then knew what the dream meant. And within a year she had died."

—Jennifer Cislo

"When I was twelve or thirteen, I dreamed that my uncle was late for a meeting. In the dream, he had his briefcase and was wearing a suit, and he got hit by a car and died. The next day, my uncle was late to a business conference, he got hit by a car as he hurried across the street, and he died. I still can't believe it."

—Movsoum Mohammed

Of course, dreaming the death of a friend or relative will make an impression on you, and some psychologists suggest that most precognitive dreams are merely examples of vivid coincidences, a few frightening images out of the thousands of images we dream each night that our minds hold onto—and then expand upon or distort in waking life.

They point out that we often dream that our loved ones are in danger or dead when they aren't, so the rare occasions when our dream images are correct should not be considered more meaningful.

Maybe.

But what about precognitive dreams that are not so earthshaking but still seem to shatter our preconceived ideas of cause and effect?

"Last year, I dreamed that my humanities professor had decided to adopt an Asian girl and was heading to Asia to pick her up. I told her and she laughed, but it was a funny kind of laugh. This year, she confessed to me that she and her husband were heading to China to adopt a baby girl, that they had just completed the paperwork on the day I had that dream, and that she was totally freaked out by this because they had told no one about it, not even their families. I have no clue as to why I should have had this dream; I've never dreamed about her before or since!"

—Dodd Bates

"I had just gotten this job at a souvenir booth at a car racing track. I had this dream the first night after I worked there. I was in the booth, and it had been broken into. I looked over at my boss, and he said, 'You know, you bust your ass for a place like this, and this is what you get!' A couple of days later, my boss called me to tell me the place had been broken into, and what did he say to me over the phone? 'You know, you bust your ass for a place like this, and this is what you get!'"

—Kent Kitzman

Anecdotes like this, of course, don't prove that psychic dreams exist. But the huge numbers of such stories and the fact that those who experience such creepy phenomena come from all walks of life with wide differences in belief and education suggest that some part of the dreaming brain is peculiarly open to transmissions from outside sources—like picking up local police activity on your transistor radio.

Dr. Robert Van De Castle, author of *Our Dreaming Mind*, asserts, "There are more ways of communicating with each other than those acknowledged by current science."

If there were some ancient channel in our brains, one that most of us are not really able to make use of except in the dream state, it might account for some of these creepy experiences. But what about shared dreams? Like this one:

> "One time, I had the same dream as a person I'm very close to. She's the only person I've ever felt really connected to, so it was indeed an odd experience. In the dream, I was walking the wrong way down the middle of a busy highway. My friend offered me a ride, but I declined. In her dream, she saw it through her eyes, she offering me the ride. The only difference was in the color of the cars. The car in my dream was black; in hers it was blue. It was weird when we discussed it because we started taking turns describing each other's private dream!"
> —Michael Housepian

Definitely weird—but possibly just a coincidence. What about this?

> "My roommate and I used to sometimes have similar dreams, and we thought it was odd but didn't make much

of it. Then, we went to Thailand for a vacation. We back-packed into the jungle and stayed in this remote village. We slept in a bamboo hut there.

"The Thais section off a part of wherever they live as a guard against evil spirits. They place attractive things in this area, which is far away from where they sleep, so that evil spirits will go there instead of bothering them in their sleep. We didn't know that, so we slept in this part of the hut, sort of like a porch, which was meant for the evil spirits. I woke up in the middle of the night completely terri-fied. Then my roommate sprang awake and asked me what was wrong. I started to describe my dream and she com-pleted every sentence because she had had the same dream! The people in our dreams were different, but the dream was the same.

"I dreamed that I was in a house with my ex-boyfriend and that as we talked, I started to feel like this was not the real guy, that there were two of him, and that this one was the bad one. I was frightened. I left the room and found the other one, and I brought him into a room and locked the door so that I could figure out what was going on. He began to speak but the words sounded all wrong!

Suddenly, his face began to peel away. His blue eyes cracked like ice and broke apart, revealing brown eyes underneath. And then I looked in the window and saw his face reflected, and I knew that I was trapped in the room with the bad one!

"In my friend's dream, it was her brother rather than her ex-boyfriend, but every other detail, down to the eyes' cracking, was exactly the same."

—Emily Harris

Some far side dream researchers suggest that shared dreams may point to the existence of an objective dream realm, an actual place, a dimension of time and space that we are aware of and can visit only when we sleep. Weird or what?

Other, somewhat more mainstream researchers insist that shared dreams are merely examples of dream telepathy, in which one of the dreamers is transmitting such a strong image that the other dreamer picks it up.

You'll be surprised to hear that I can't answer this question for you! Not enough research has been done on the far side of dreams yet for any real conclusions. But dream telepathy has been studied, and a good case has been made for it by highly respectable (if peculiar) scientists.

The most famous of these dream telepathy projects was a series of experiments carried out at the Maimonides Dream Laboratory, in Brooklyn during the late 1960s by the renowned dream researchers Dr. Montague Ullman and Dr. Stanley Krippner.

Here's how the experiments worked. Three people were involved: one the sender, the second the receiver or percipient of the dream image, and a third to monitor the experiment.

The receiver went to sleep in a locked, sound-insulated bedroom, and his or her sleep stages were monitored on an EEG. The sender slept in a similar chamber far removed from the receiver. The monitor kept track of the receiver's sleep cycle through the EEG. When the receiver went into REM sleep, the monitor woke the sender, and the sender attempted to transmit an image to the receiver by concentrating on it during the period of the receiver's REM sleep. The image was randomly selected from paintings and prints. The same image was used throughout the night, and no one but the sender ever knew what it was.

After fifteen minutes of REM activity, the monitor woke the receiver and asked him to describe his dreams in as much detail as possible. The dream reports were taped. This procedure went on throughout the night, each time the receiver went into a REM state.

The next day—and they must have been pretty tired!—the sender would question the receiver on what she remembered about the dreams. Then the receiver would be shown eight possible target pictures and asked to rank them (one through eight) according to which the receiver felt came closest to the images she had seen in dreams. The receiver was also asked to rate her confidence level (one through one hundred) in terms of how closely it matched the content or emotions of her dreams.

Sounds complicated, doesn't it? But the study had remarkable successes, like this one.

One of the target pictures was *The Sacrament of the Last Supper* by Salvador Dali, a vivid version of the last supper, in which Jesus is at the center of the table, surrounded by his disciples. There is a glass of wine and a loaf of bread on the table. The sea is in the background, with a fishing boat off in the distance.

One of the percipients, Dr. William Erwin, first dreamed about the ocean. In his second dream, he reported that fishing boats and a picture of twelve men hauling in a catch came to his mind. In his third dream he was looking through a Christmas catalogue. His following three dreams were about doctors. His last two dreams of the night were about food.

The next morning, reflecting upon these images, Dr. Erwin said that his dreams made him think of "the Mediterranean area, perhaps even some sort of Biblical time. Right now, my associations are of the fish and the loaf, even the feeding of the multitudes . . . Christmas."

He easily selected the reproduction of the Dali painting as the image closest in spirit to his dreams.

Of the twelve studies completed from 1966 to 1972, nine showed considerable accuracy between the images sent and the images received, far higher than mere coincidence would suggest. Further studies during the 1970s and 1980s at Maimonides had an accuracy rating of 83.5 percent. The odds of this occurring by chance are about 250,000 to 1.

Dr. Stephen LaBerge, the pioneer of lucid dreaming, says, "The findings of the Maimonides research offer scientific support for the possibility of telepathic influence on dream content."

But what's the explanation?

Jan Tolaas, a Norwegian dream scholar, suggests that many of these creepy reports may point to some kind of "preverbal emergency channel," a part of our brains buried by the evolution of language. Perhaps this secret channel is accessed more easily in the dream state because the dream state behaves much more like pre-verbal consciousness, full of image and activity and metaphors and symbols.

Plausible?

I have no clue myself, but maybe you'll find a clue. And maybe your clue will lead you through what Havelock Ellis called "the opaque curtain," which separates the present from the future, and on to the far side of dreams.

First Dream It—Then Do It

OK, the next project is going to take a little organizing, and it's going to take someone else to help you out, but with a little effort (and some interrupted sleep) you can try a modified version of the Maimonides experiments.

1. You'll need to have a sender and a receiver, that is, you and an associate. Your associate needs to be someone you can trust or someone who won't think you're (totally) nuts, so

make your brother or sister or best friend be part of this little
experiment. You should probably alternate roles.

2. If possible, get a third person to help you out, too. Ask that
person to choose five or so pictures. They can be photos or
prints or reproductions of paintings—they can be about
almost anything, but bright and vivid is better than black and
white. The sender could choose the images himself, but that
would raise the possibility of his inadvertently letting the
receiver know what the image is.

3. Put all the images in envelopes and let the sender randomly
select one of the images. Since you probably don't have an
EEG at home and since your folks probably won't like it if
you stay up all night to do this, you'll need to set up specific
times when the receiver will sleep and the sender will not.

4. The sender must concentrate for at least fifteen minutes on
the picture, really concentrate on it, and try to imagine sending that picture through the air to the receiver. The receiver
needs to at least accept the possibility that this will work and
needs also to agree to set an alarm so he can wake up at a
preordained time and write down (or better yet, tell into a
tape recorder) what he remembers of his dreams that night.

5. You probably should do the same image over several nights, but—and here's the hard part—the sender must try not to give any hint of what the picture is to the receiver.

6. After a predecided period (say, three nights), you and your associate should sit down together and compare notes. The sender should show the receiver all five of the images and see which one the receiver feels comes closest to the dream images.

7. Not everyone is open to this weirdness, so you might need to experiment with several people before you find someone with whom you feel comfortable doing this. Try to keep good records, and then go back and check on how often you and your friends came close to the image.

Remember, even if dream telepathy exists, it's not like a telephone call; the images need not be exact and the descriptions need not be scientifically precise for there to be a suggestion of success.

Obviously, this is only an approximation of the more elaborate experiments we talked about. But it might work, and it might lead you to some new conclusions about the power of dreams, the power of suggestion, and the power of your own creativity.

So, try it!

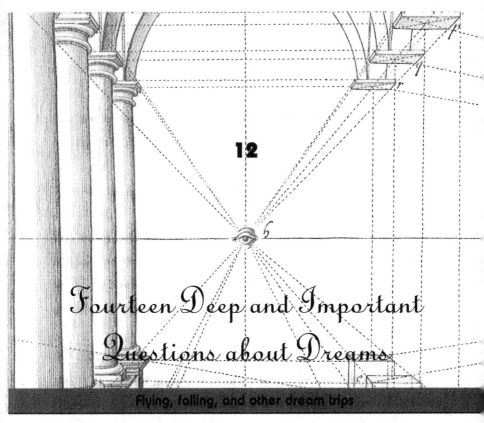

12

Fourteen Deep and Important Questions about Dreams

Flying, falling, and other dream trips

We've dashed across a fair amount of ground already—ancient Greece, Native Americans, Freud, Jung. Totally weird stuff!

We have a lot more to talk about, but before we do, I thought it might be a good time for us to *Stop! Look Around!* and ask you to provide a few answers of your own.

So, take a few minutes, if you would, and fill out this questionnaire. I won't be collecting these at the end of the period (though you could send it to me if you like). Nobody but you will read it (unless you want them to). Nobody but you will know what you really see in your world of dreams (unless you decide to start a dream group, which isn't a bad idea!).

This is not a test—but it might give you a chance to really decide what you think.

The great American short story writer Flannery O'Connor said that she was the sort of writer who didn't know what she thought about a subject until she saw what she had written about it. That's how I feel much of the time, and maybe you feel that way about a lot of the dream material we've been discussing.

I came up with this questionnaire when I first started to think about writing this book (it was a way of avoiding writing it, really, but that's another story), and I subsequently asked my students and many of my former students to fill it out for me. Most of them did, and I've already quoted some of their responses throughout this book.

But because many of them had such interesting things to say about their dreams, I thought I'd include a more or less random sampling of some of their responses in this chapter. Some

> *"The dream . . . is a message of yourself to yourself."*
>
> *—Fritz Perls*

of the questions have already gotten some attention earlier or will later, so I'm skimming over them here, OK?

So, first, fill out the questionnaire yourself. Second, read what some other people had to say about the same subjects.

It's no fair jumping ahead and reading what they said first. Let your own ideas and images and vague notions spill out—they're just as important and interesting as anything in this book!

First Dream It—Then Do It

Stephen's Dream Questionnaire

1. Do you usually/sometimes/hardly ever remember your dreams? When you do remember them, how do they make you feel? Do they make you laugh, make you shudder, make you feel uneasy? Try to write a few sentences about your general feelings about your own dreams.

2. Are dreams ever discussed in your family? Among your friends? What can you think of that someone has told you

about dreams (e.g., "I always heard dreams were just gibber-ish and nonsense" or "You know, if you dream about flying it means you're dreaming about sex" or whatever)?

3. Do you feel like you understand your dreams? Do you feel like they are mostly nonsense? Have you ever had a dream (or a series of dreams) that seemed important to you?

4. Have you ever had recurring dreams? If so, what were they like? Why do you think you had these dreams?

5. What do your dreams look like to you? Are they in color? (Always? Never?) Do they look more or less like reality? Like some weird *Alice in Wonderland* world?

6. Are you always (or often) in your dreams, or more often just observing them? Are your dreams mostly about people? Objects? Who or what populates your dreams mostly?

7. Have you ever dreamed about flying? Falling? Being chased by a monster? Briefly, describe these dreams if you can.

8. Have you ever had a dream that really bothered you? If you can, describe it. Do you have any thoughts about what it meant?

9. Many people feel that dreams offer us insight into our feel-ings, our problems, or our lives; others feel that dreams are

rarely worth thinking about. What's your opinion?

10. Have you ever felt like you had a premonition or psychic experience in a dream? Please describe it if you can.

11. Do you ever discuss your dreams with anyone? If so, who, and what kind of reaction do you get? Do you ever write your dreams down?

12. Have you ever had a dream that helped solve a problem or inspired you to create something or worked on you in some other intangible way? Please say something about this, if you can.

13. Some people have a fairly vivid memory of a dream from childhood; if you do, please describe it briefly.

14. If you were given the opportunity, would you stop dreaming? Dream more? Learn more about your dreams? Never think about them again . . . or what?

What Some Other People Said

Here are responses to some of the questions in my dream questionnaire.

Q1. Do you usually/sometimes/hardly ever remember your dreams?

"I usually remember my dreams, yet this is a recent development. I've trained myself. They generally leave me feeling uneasy. The plots are muddled and confused! Yet, since I've been writing them down, the pictures have become clearer."

—Jessica Tollner

"There are times when I'll be at work, sitting at my desk, and something wholly arbitrary triggers some kind of release valve in my dream tank and the previous night's dreams spill all over everything. I like it—it's sort of like being hypnotized."

—Dakota Shepard

"I rarely remember my dreams but when I do, I feel a certain relief because sometimes I wake up with a sensation that I did dream and it bothers me that I can't remember what it was I dreamed."

—Robert Conde

Q3. Do you feel like you understand your dreams?

"For the most part, I understand my dreams, though I can't always put their meaning into words. Sometimes, my understanding is as abstract as the images of the dream are."

—Jennifer Cislo

"I don't feel like I understand my dreams, but they often do reflect what is on my mind—things I don't express in words."

—Asmina Pertesis

"At first I think my dreams are nonsense, until I really sit down to think. Then I feel they have something to tell me; often they show my stress or my anticipation of something."

—Mari Flannery

"I don't try to understand my dreams. They make sense to me on a very visceral level. They affect me, but not in a coherent way. I know what they're about in the same way I know what my life is about and my heart. But I couldn't tell you—it would all come out as lies."

—Michelle Tupko

Q4. Have you ever had recurring dreams?

"I had a recurring dream that the walls of my new room were closing in on me. After I got used to my room, they stopped."

—Robert Conde

"When I was ten, I had a recurring dream. I am walking on a wall, beneath me are shrubs. I lose my balance and fall, and as I'm falling the shrubs turn into a pit of alligators—scary!"

—Tiffany Moy

"I used to have a recurring dream in which I was at an intersection of a busy street in my hometown, Chicago. I looked in both directions and didn't know which way to go. I feel panic, that I'm lost, but at the same time I know I'm not lost because I've seen this street so many times before. Possibly, this dream is about my difficulty making decisions. To make a choice is to close off options, but not to choose is just to stand there, immobilized by fear."

—Lyndee Yamshon

"I have two recurring dreams, and members of my family have reported the same dreams! 1. We are trapped in a black sedan on top of a bridge. My grandfather is driving;

we are all screaming. 2. There is a sunny field. The female spinster character from *The Beverly Hillbillies* is standing in a tweed suit. She is laughing as she grinds a giant meat grinder with a human mouth!"

—Jessica Tollner

"I have one recurring dream where I am in this creepy movie house, and I watch whole movies. They start with credits, have form, and seem to last long, like real movies!"

—Dodd Bates

Q5. What do your dreams look like to you? Are they in color?

"My dreams are usually in color and quite realistic. Once in a while, though, they look like an acid trip—water sparkling too brightly and people's faces too detailed and grotesque. These dreams can be fun but more often than not, they turn into nightmares."

—Dakota Shepard

"Color. Fractals. Bright—as if every surface were slide-projected. As if paintings came to life. Light is the visual key in my dreams."

—Adriane Vawter

"My dreams are very vivid and usually surrealistic. They are almost always in color, but there is usually a scheme of color or one prominent color. The things that are different in my dreams in comparison to reality are my reactions, my thought processes. Things that should be taken lightly become very intense emotionally."

—Tara Peyman

"The color in my dreams is especially strong. I've always had this love for expressionist art—Van Gogh, Kokoscha, and so forth—and I think it's because it reminds me of my dreams or links them to my subconscious mind."

—Sarah Kendzior

Q6. Are you always (or often) in your dreams, or more often just observing them?

"I am almost always in my dreams, although I rarely look like myself. Sometimes, I am even a guy, but the dreams are still from my point of view. Sometimes, I am observing my dreams, and occasionally I even catch a little glimpse of myself observing them."

—Pelin Batu

"I am usually in my dreams as myself—sometimes at various stages of my life. I am also an observer, a narrator."
—Jessica Daponte

"I'm usually in my dreams—but the girl doesn't always look like me!"
—Adrienne Mason

"Animals figure prominently in my dreams."
—Dakota Shepard

"I often dream in phases of topics—like for a week, I'll dream about fire; then for a few days I'll dream about glass."
—Tara Peyman

Q7. Have you ever dreamed about flying? Falling?

"To fly in my dreams I have to sort of swing and push; it's like riding a bike. It's so much fun! In these dreams, I fly through the woods and reservoir I live near."
—Adriane Vawter

"As a child, I dreamed that when I flew, the trees were my friends and would catch me if I lost control. Then, awake,

I almost fell off a balcony because I believed this and
wanted to join my friends, as I had in my dream."
—Kate Soukhapalov

"I don't fly, but I often float in my dreams. I stand still, and
concentrate, and just float up into the sky; I can glide on
wind or walk around in the air. It's weird, because I can't
stay there. I settle down to earth, eventually, and sometimes I try and try and just can't float."
—Khristian Kemp-DeLisser

Q8. Have you ever had a dream that really bothered you?

"I constantly dream about death. I dreamed I saw my dad
commit suicide; other times I've dreamed I was at his
funeral. Once, in a dream, I spoke with my grandfather,
who died when I was three, and he was telling me about
heaven. These dreams all disturbed me, but I think I
dream about death so much because there's been so much
death in my family."
—Jamie Altman

"One dream that really bothered me was of my own death.
Blood was draining from my body and I was turning blue.

There was nobody there to help me. I had actually been in the hospital for internal bleeding just before this, and the doctor told me after surgery I had been in real danger. In the dream, I looked at myself in the mirror and was so frightened! I felt incredible helplessness. It upset me for days."

—Sabrina Panfilo

"The most disturbing dream I ever had was of moving from Illinois to upstate New York, when I was ten. It was a simple but vivid picture of my mother and me standing inside a school in upstate New York. I realized she was registering me to go to this new school. I was terribly scared and angry. And it came true. Shortly after that, we moved to upstate New York, and my mother and I soon stood in that same school. It was not an abstract likeness, but an exact portrait of the school. I have never forgotten it."

—Glenn Williams

"My dreams so often scare me that I think sometimes I might like to stop dreaming!"

—Jessica Tomb

Q9. Many people feel that dreams offer us insight into our feelings, our problems, or our lives; others feel that dreams are
rarely worth thinking about. What's your opinion?

"I believe dreams offer plenty of insight into the feelings
we're not always willing to look at. Dreaming is the cure
for a life confined by jobs, houses, and law."
    —Dakota Shepard

"To me, dreams hold as much value as one's waking
moments."
    —Glenn Williams

"Not all my dreams seem significant or important, but I
strongly believe we can learn from the unconscious."
    —Y. Lee

"In a way, I trust my dreams and think they offer more
than my rational daylight thinking."
    —Jennifer Cislo

"Most people spend their lives thinking about what time
the bus is, what's for dinner, and so on. Dreaming may be
the only chance they have to let that go and use other parts

of the brain. And if the mind chooses to remember those strange midnight flashes of terror and bliss, there must be a damn good reason!"

—Michelle Tupko

"Some dreams seem to offer insights; others just stir my thoughts up! Maybe they show us stuff about ourselves we may not want to admit, like the parts of us that don't quite fit with the way we act on the outside."

—Billy Maitland

Q14. If you were given the opportunity, would you stop dreaming? Dream more?

"I almost always hate my dreams, but I wouldn't give them up for anything in the world."

—Michael Housepian

"I love being other people and a stranger version of myself! In fact, if there were a surgical procedure that could cause you to dream more, I'd do it—for the good of science and my own entertainment."

—Kate Soukhapalov

"I would never wish to stop dreaming. Dreaming is what provides me with all the energy in the morning when I never want to leave my bed. It's my world—only mine."
—Pelin Batu

"If I could, I would never wake up."
—Adriane Vawter

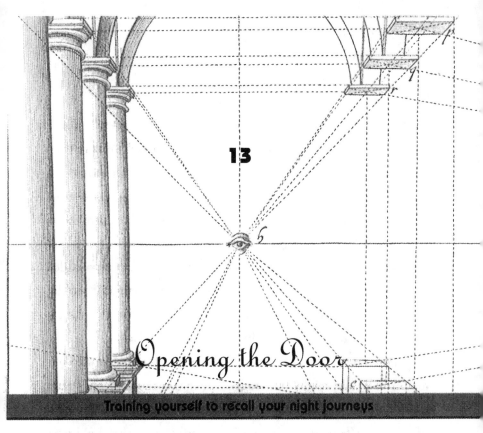

13

Opening the Door

Training yourself to recall your night journeys

$\mathcal{I}$n the remaining chapters of this book, we're going to consider a few ways of trying to make sense of these often nonsensical narratives of the night, and we'll take a look, too, at some of the ways in which people have made creative use of their dreams.

But this will be of no real use to you if you can't remember your dreams in the first place! So, let's see what can be done about that age-old cry: "I never remember my dreams!"

It may seem to you from reading this book that everyone in the world but you has easy access to their unconscious. That isn't true. It is true, of course, that some people seem to have less difficulty recalling their dreamworlds than others do, just as there are some people who can do algebra more easily than others and some people who have better singing voices than others.

But even people who regularly consult the unconscious don't always recall their dreams—I often go for weeks without recalling much, and then I will enter a strangely fertile period of dream recall and remember several dreams a night for a week.

When are we most likely to recall our dreams? The door to our dream life will probably be nudged open a bit more when we are in a dilemma, such as feeling unresolved about a friendship or a life choice. We may also be moving closer to that threshold when we are in a new situation, or traveling, or experiencing some major (or even minor) change in our routines.

In other words, any time your conscious mind is receiving new sensory information appears to be a good time to try befriending your dream process.

When is dream recall most difficult? Well, not getting enough sleep doesn't help much, and making yourself feel compelled to recall your dreams isn't useful, either.

But there are lots of reasons and many theories for why we don't recall our dreams. According to J. Allan Hobson, the chemical that is used for imprinting information in our memories is switched off during sleep, so if we do not recount to ourselves what we dreamed as soon as we wake up (when the memory chemical switches back on), the images will be lost, washed out of our thoughts like ink in a rainstorm.

Some dreams may be simply too bizarre, too frightening, too unlike our waking world to be apprehended and recalled by the brain. Alcohol and a wide variety of drugs have been shown to suppress REM sleep, which makes us less likely to experience vivid dreaming and to recall dreams, as well.

Then, too, sometimes wanting too much to succeed at a task is the very cause of our failing to do it. Like writer's block, we can get dreamer's block by pushing ourselves too hard.

But most people can learn to recall some of their dreams if they want to, if they relax and let their unconscious do the work. Here are some suggestions:

1. *Annoy everyone you know by telling them what you're doing.*

Tell your friends that you're trying to remember your dreams. Some may yawn and say, "Yeah, so?" but a few might get interested, and then you'll have a whole bunch of people trying to do these exercises, which is more fun.

Tell your siblings, tell your folks, or tell your teachers if you like and trust them. Sure, a few of these people will say, "Are you quite all right, dear?" But one of these people might surprise you by having experience in working with dreams and may be able to inspire you.

The act of talking about dreams in our waking life is sometimes enough to increase our actual recall of dreams. Just reading this book may help you, too. Whenever I've read Freud, I've had Freudian dreams; reading Jung often seems to evoke myth-type dreams. The unconscious is more suggestible than you might think!

2. *Repetition rules!*

Set yourself a specific period of time (say, a week), and every night for that week repeat to yourself forty-nine times, "I will remember a dream tonight" (yes, it has to be forty-nine times). Say it as you are brushing your teeth or lying in bed listening to the radio. Say it like you mean it—but not desperately.

If you keep a journal, write it every night in your journal. If you don't keep a journal, write it on your computer, say it into a tape recorder, or shout it out the window (but if the police show up, don't tell them I suggested this).

What we want to do here is to leave that door between the unconscious and the conscious ajar. The more you emphasize to yourself how real and important this task is, the more likely you are to find that door has been pushed open.

3. *Visualize! Visualize! Visualize!*

After you've bored yourself to tears by repeating the resolution above, relax, close your eyes, and try to picture yourself waking up from a dream, remembering it, and writing it down. Narrate to yourself what you see, for example, "I see myself coming out of a dream, I see myself grasping on to my pillow, I see myself smiling as I realize I've remembered my dream, I see myself recounting the dream, remembering even more. . . ."

If you manage to see yourself succeeding at this task, it may actually improve your chances for success.

4. *The right tools help!*

Almost everyone has had the experience of recalling a dream as they awaken only to have it slip utterly away as they walk to the bathroom. In a study of dream recall techniques, one group of dreamers was asked to call local weather information before they tried to recall a dream while a second group was asked to write down their dream memories immediately. Which group would you guess remembered significantly more of their dreams?

OK, so you need to have a pad and pen or a tape recorder (voice activated would be the best) right next to your bed. Don't think that you'll get up and go to your desk—you won't! Don't worry about penmanship or whether you're using the most poetic language or whether your voice sounds like you've gargled with pebbles, just get as much down as you can as quickly as you can.

Pay particular attention to any words, phrases, songs, colors, sensations that seem to be in your thoughts as you wake up. You might want to lie there with your eyes closed before you jump up. Let the dream images wash over you (but don't go back to sleep!).

If the dream seems terribly vague and elusive, you might try running through a list of your friends, loved ones, family members, people important in your life; try visualizing their faces. Chances are your dream included one or more of these important people, and running your thoughts over them may help loosen the dream associations.

Dream expert Patricia Garfield suggests trying to write your dreams down with your eyes closed. You might wish to try this, though personally, I always feel too clumsy to do it that way. I get self-conscious and thus lose the thread I'm trying to grasp at.

It also helps to tell someone your dream as soon after awakening as possible. If you've managed to con a friend or sister into working with you, telling her the dream in as much detail as you can will help fix it in your conscious mind.

5. *Honor the irrational.*

Don't try to analyze your dreams as you recall them and don't fret that they are simply too bizarre for words (or too stupid or not creative enough). Just try to let them flow out of you. You might try freewriting. After you've written down even a fragment of a dream, set yourself a very brief period of time, like two minutes. Write down an image or phrase you recall (e.g., "stranger in red dress") over and over until some associations start to pop into your head.

Write without stopping for your set time; if you hesitate, go back to the initial phrase. You may find that some additional images or pieces of the dream puzzle come to you as you are writing.

6. *Fool yourself!*

If all else fails, set your alarm clock for about forty-five minutes before you usually get up. This itself may help you by interrupting your REM sleep cycle. If not, turn off the alarm and go back to sleep for half an hour. You will be more likely to recall a dream at this stage, because you will be in a shallower part of the dream cycle.

If none of these things work, try to forget all about dream recall. Go on reading this book and, if you like, jump ahead to the list at the end and read some dream-related stories or look at some dream-related artwork. Decide that you aren't going to try and recall your dreams, but continue to read, think, and eat, drink, and sleep dreams. Eventually, you will almost certainly recall some part of some dream, and the more you start to appreciate your own unconscious, the wider the doorway will be to your dreamworld.

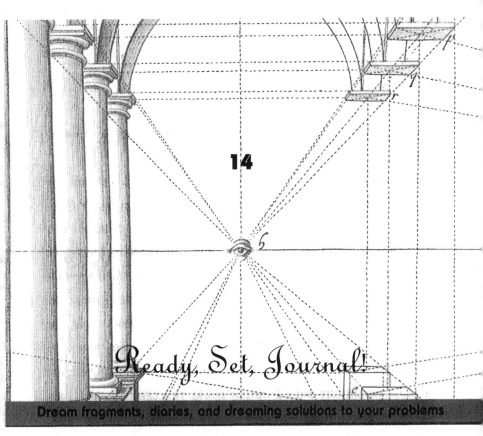

14

Ready, Set, Journal!

Dream fragments, diaries, and dreaming solutions to your problems

You've managed to start recalling fragments of your dreams now, and some mornings you even wake up with dreams almost whole in your head as if they were still a presence. Now what?

Well, there are a lot of responses to that question ("Get a life!" some might respond—though not me). One of the best I know is: start a dream journal.

You may be following my advice and jotting down your dream

fragments as you wake up, and while that's the first step toward keeping a dream journal, it's not quite the same.

In a dream journal (or log, or diary, or record, or sketchbook, or whatever you want to call it), you elaborate on the dream fragments, you rewrite them so that you can understand them later, and you make some order out of them, possibly adding your later thoughts on what they might mean (which we'll—finally!—talk about in Chapter 15), how they relate to your waking life, how they relate to previous dreams, or what kinds of associations you have to them. A dream journal may be just a section of your day-to-day diary, or it may be a separate record. It may be kept in one of those beautifully bound leather books you can buy at a fancy stationery store, in an old notebook, on a sketch pad, or on disk, for that matter.

First Dream It—Then Do It

There is no right or wrong way to keep a dream journal, but there are some things to consider as you begin.

1. *Don't wait too long!*

The strange scratchy handwriting you produce to recall your dreams in the morning will look even less comprehensible in a few days, so transfer your dreams into your dream journal as soon as you can.

2. *Smooth out the edges.*

This time, it's OK to write out your dreams in slightly less rough style, to try to find the right words, the best way of phrasing what you recall. But try not to change the dream, and try not to elaborate so much that you're actually inventing (that's a whole different, equally interesting ball game, which is coming up in Chapter 18).

You probably will find that as you rewrite the dream, you remember more of it. If so, you should probably make note of the fact that this is a later recall of the dream from the previous night. That way, you can see later on how much of your dream presented itself immediately and how much needed to be prodded before it made its appearance.

3. *Don't skip any dreams, even the silly ones.*

Remember, the unconscious works in peculiar ways, and sometimes the dreams that seem to us to make the least sense, to be the most elusive, fragmentary, or downright childish, may contain the seed of some new self-knowledge (or at least some fine entertainment). You should write down everything that you remember about every dream, regardless of how foolish it may make you feel. This dream diary will not be shown to your future dates, the admissions department of your favorite college, or the FBI, so try to be as faithful to the dreams as you can be— they will repay you with insight or at least laughter.

4. *Don't editorialize.*

You almost certainly will find that you have something to say about your dreams after you start really paying attention to them, but it's helpful to write the dreams down fully first and then write your comments. If you interrupt the flow of your dream entry with interpretations or associations, you may never get to the end of the dream. (On the other hand, this is your dream journal; if you can't keep yourself from making associations as you write down the dream or if you find yourself turning the dream into a television sitcom pilot, or anything else, that's up to you!)

Once you've got the dream on paper, it might be useful to write down immediately anything else you think about in association with the dream or anything odd about the dream. You might also want to note or underline the parts of the dream that seemed hardest to see, recall, or understand.

5. *Record all the important information.*

Be sure to write the date somewhere in each dream entry. If you can recall at what point in the night the dream occurred, write that down, too. If you can recall how you felt as you were drifting off to sleep that night or what was in your thoughts, you might wish to include that data, as well.

Dream expert Dr. Patricia Garfield suggests you give each dream entry a title—say, one of the most provocative images from the dream (e.g., Giant Tomato Dream, January 5, 1997). That way, if you ever decide to spend some time considering the most common (or most peculiar) images in your dreams, you'll be able to locate them.

6. *Ask your unconscious.*

A dream journal is a good place to try dream incubation. What is that? Basically, "dream incubation" is asking your unconscious to give you a dream on a specific subject or a dream that will help you solve a problem or understand how you truly feel about someone. It's a smaller version of the techniques the ancient Greeks used when they asked for healing dreams in the snake-filled temple of Asclepius.

If you want to try this, write down the question in simple language in your dream journal just before you go to bed, for example, "Dear Journal, tonight I would like to have a dream that will help me understand why my sister and I fight all the time" or "Dear Unconscious, tonight please help me dream the answer to my hangup on that weirdo who lives next door."

After you write your dream incubation down, repeat it to yourself as you lie in bed. When you recall your dreams the next morning, do not try and decipher how the dream relates to your question at first; just record it. Then, as you enter it into your dream journal, write the question down again, and then write down the dream.

Do the dreams that you recall address the question you asked? Are there any references—even obscure ones—to the person or experience you were brooding about?

Remember that the unconscious often speaks to us in metaphors, so a dream that may seem to have little to do with what you asked about may still have a connection to your question.

Dream incubation is tricky, though. Sometimes, the unconscious just doesn't feel like obliging us!

7. *Don't be hung up on words.*

There are many ways to keep a dream journal. If you are not necessarily a writing person, you might try sketching your dreams. Remember, we are not asking for great art here, just anything that will allow you to continue seeing what your unconscious eyes perceived in the dream. Doodles, cartoons, even cutouts can help you keep track of your dreams. An actress I know used to cut pictures out of magazines and paste them into her dream diary to help her visualize the jumble of her dreamworld (OK, she had a lot of free time, but it's not a bad idea).

To help you get started on this next phase of your dream voyage, I'm including here a few excerpts from other people's dream journals, the weird yet strangely appealing log of their night journeys.

" . . . I had a dream of my grandmother. I walked into this alley where old women were baking bread and knitting. I spotted my grandmother and grabbed her hand. I was then walking on a brick wall or barrier. My grandmother was below me and she was holding my hand. I asked her repeatedly, 'Why did you have to go?' I said, 'I feel like I have no one to talk to, like I am not my whole self, the self I used to be.'

"My grandmother tried to convince me that this is the way it's supposed to be and that if she knew I could not handle life on my own, she would not have left. The last thing I remember saying is, 'Don't go. Don't leave me again.' I don't know what happened then; I guess I woke up.

"There are two odd things about this dream: (1) In the dream, I was dreaming about my grandmother, it was a dream about dreaming, and I knew that I was dreaming about her and (2) I was missing in the dream. People were looking for me, and I wound up in this alley and found my grandmother. But in the dream, I was never found. . . ."

—Sabrina Panfilo

"Tried incubation. Asked my unconscious for a dream about my boyfriend; was I ready for this relationship? Had a weird dream. Was trapped in a fast-food restaurant with someone I can't picture, but he was my partner in the dream. Some guys were chasing us, and we were running around the place in suits made out of birds' wings. We were going to jump out the window, because the suits would let us fly. We jumped, but I had a hard time, couldn't fly, and landed in the water, but that was cool because I turned into a fish. My partner was gone, but I met a few friends in the water and they told me how they love to tease the fisherman and I should try it. So, I found this guy, the fisherman, and I played with his fishing line. He got angry and yelled, 'I'm going to get you!' Then he turned into a fish and was chasing me, but I turned back into a person and pushed his face away and kept pushing it and pushing it away. Not sure what the dream meant. Did my incubation work?

"[much later] I think the dream is telling me that I'm not ready for what he wants. The whole fish/fisherman thing seemed very sexual!"

—Anita Gill

"I have been dreaming a great deal lately about clothing!

"Dream #25: Amber sends me a present since she feels guilty for not calling for such a long time. It's in red wrapping paper, and I tear it apart to find a cushion with little sketches on it. The first picture is of a girl, and when Diane comes over, she tells me that the girl looks awfully like me. It is only then that I realize that all the little pictures are stories about me. In the background, I hear a song that goes, 'As I lay me down to sleep. . . .'

"Dream #27: My grandmother comes back and brings my brother a 'mountain' jacket with a million pockets. It's white and yellow. It's not the best thing, but I am jealous because he gets something and I do not. We take an airplane, except that we are not really in a plane; our seats are outside somehow; they fly by themselves. We fly through these strange red stone tunnels. We go through seven or eight chambers with immense speed. During the dream, I think we are in some Inca or Aztec sacred place.

"The tunnels get smaller, and we get smaller as we descend. (As I write this, I think that recently reading Dante's *Inferno* might have affected this dream.)"

—Pelin Batu

"Before I began recording these dreams, I could never recall any actual plot. I could see no one clearly. The dreams were remembered as grainy black-and-white snapshots from which I always woke confused. However, now that I keep this journal, I am recalling actual color, sound, and faces!

"The most surprising thing I've noted is the series of physical sensations I experience nightly. In some dreams, my eyes hurt and I can't see much; in others there is a constant sense of sorrow.

"The landscape of my dreams seems always to be a mixture of the prairie of northern Illinois, the East Village of New York, and backstage at a religious television network. Every dream seems to share these settings, no matter what the plot may be!

"I am glad I began this documentation, for I have gained much insight into. . . . Well, I'm not quite sure, but it's fascinating none the less."

—Jessica Tollner

As you can see, each approach is a little different; each journal voice is personal, idiosyncratic. These dream questers do it their own way.

So, come on! Find the right kind of journal (very important—it must feel right for you and your unconscious!) and start your own log of weirdness.

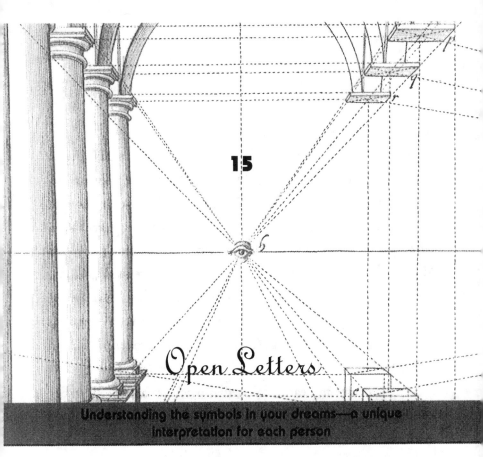

15

Open Letters

*I*magine receiving a letter that has no return address on it, so you aren't sure who sent it to you. Getting a letter like this causes you to get a mysterious feeling. Maybe you're dying to rip the letter open immediately and see who wrote you and why, or maybe you hold the envelope and examine it very carefully. You might be just a little bit apprehensive about opening the letter—

after all, it could contain bad news.

There is a famous proverb from the Talmud, the medieval book of Jewish wisdom, that states, "A dream that has not been understood is like a letter that has not been opened." This states the case for working toward understanding your dreams very clearly. We've already seen that many people—both experts and amateurs—view dreams as a sort of letter from one part of ourselves to the other, a conversation we're having with our unconscious. And even if you're a little apprehensive, you're still going to want to open that letter eventually, aren't you? A letter needs to be opened; a dream needs to be understood. But how do we understand them?

It's important to bear in mind that when we talk about understanding our dreams, it isn't quite the same as understanding a mathematical equation or even making sense of a sentence in a foreign language. Dreams are understood in a more intuitive way; it's rare to be able to understand a dream precisely, with no elusive or mysterious qualities to it. Dreams are, by their very nature, elusive and mysterious, and our understanding of them can rarely be a total understanding.

But how do we understand them?

Many books exist that will give you very precise answers to that question, offering a whole list of dream symbols and what they mean ("If you dream of a crab, beware of jealous colleagues"). But as you've already guessed, this isn't one of those books.

Instead, in the next few chapters, we're going to look at a few of the elements that seem to account for much of the content of our dreams and pose some questions you might want to ask yourself about some of the dream pictures your unconscious may be painting, the dream tales your unconscious may be spinning.

There are, of course, some dream images and narratives that don't require a lot of effort to make sense of, or at least to establish a feeling of connection to. Classic anxiety dreams, which are sometimes referred to as "student dreams" or "performance dreams," are like that. For example, you are on your way to take an exam (or you're sitting at your desk, or you're in a car on the way to school). It occurs to you that you haven't actually been to this class all year, you haven't studied, and you have no idea what the exam will be about. Or, you are about to go on stage in a play (or in the school band, or in a dance recital). You've never been to rehearsal, you don't know your lines, and you're not even sure what the play is that you're supposed to be performing.

These dreams are sometimes really about being a student and taking exams, but more often that situation is just a metaphor for some other part of your life about which you feel uncertain. The message is fairly clear: you haven't done your job, you haven't taken care of business, you are unprepared—or, just as likely, you are simply worried about whether you're up to a task and your unconscious is reflecting that worry.

When you're actually a student experiencing student anxiety dreams, it doesn't seem so unusual, but many people go on experiencing such anxiety dreams well into adulthood, years and years after they stopped taking exams, were last in a school play, or packed away their clarinet.

In my early twenties, I had a similar recurring dream scenario, which I used to call academy dreams, in reference to the private military school I attended from fifth through twelfth grades (don't ask!). In these dreams, I was late for drill, my shoes weren't shined, I couldn't find my rifle, I couldn't find where the drill was taking place, or there was a parade and I was late for it. Years and years after I last had to perform the noxious task of marching in Memorial Day parades in my dress uniform, I continued to dream about it whenever I was in an anxiety state about something in my life or felt that I did not fit in with my surroundings.

Why? The dream images that kept recurring showed me in what might have been one of my least comfortable roles, in one of my least favorite activities. I was a largely incompetent cadet, and

I loathed doing it; I felt awkward, stupid, vulnerable, as so many people do in their high school years (this is not a surprise to you, I'm guessing).

So, whenever I brushed up against those feelings in adult life, the same images would be thrust forward from my unconscious, as if to say, "You may think you have outgrown this feeling of awkwardness, but you haven't."

Certain other anxiety images fall into this category, too:

• Dreams where you can't move or speak, for instance, can often be understood as suggesting that you feel stuck or unable to accomplish something, that you are not being heard, or that you have been too silent on a subject of importance.

• Dreams that you are lost may be offering the obvious message that you have lost your way, that you have lost some part of you that you value, or that part of you feels as if you are heading in a wrong direction.

• Dreams that your teeth (or some other body part) are loose or falling out (a very common anxiety dream) probably refer to a fear that you are not in control of your life. Think how vulnerable we would be if we did lose our teeth—unable to eat, unable to talk, we would be essentially powerless.

Of course, not every dream in which these images occur means the same thing, but many people who have these dreams, if

"But he would have us remember most of all

To be enthusiastic over the night...."

—*W. H. Auden*

they allow themselves to run their minds over the images, would be able to say, "I have a feeling this dream was not about my teeth but about..." whatever may be bothering them that they have not, perhaps, fully acknowledged.

The poet W. H. Auden said, "Learn from your dreams what you lack." Anxiety dreams seem a strong example of that. You may already know what this kind of dream is about without ever having to interpret it.

And even if some elements don't seem to relate to the main thrust of the dream, that does not invalidate the feeling that you understand this dream even though you aren't necessarily able to say exactly what it all means.

Let me give you an example from my own dream journal.

In September 1995, my wife and I adopted a baby, and I had a series of dreams during the preceding summer that all seemed to be related to my anxieties and tremendous anticipation about this exciting event.

The day before I had the dream I am about to recount, an old college friend of mine and his wife visited us from California with their baby. I quizzed my friend on his perceptions of fatherhood, and we talked a bit about whether he had felt prepared for it and how unprepared I felt. Several other college friends joined us later for dinner.

This is the dream:

> I am filled with a great unease. I am with Jim (a college friend, but not one of the ones I'd just seen); we are on our way to a theater. Apparently, I am playing Hamlet at this theater, only the production has been on some kind of hiatus and during that time I haven't bothered to rehearse or even look at the script. Jim tells me that this is not a good idea. "I've acted like that, and it didn't turn out so well," he tells me. "You need to prepare."
>
> In particular, I'm concerned about the soliloquy that starts "Oh, what a rogue and peasant slave am I," and as we get to the theater, I realize that I don't know the next line, that I'm totally unprepared to perform Hamlet.
>
> Jim goes to sit in the theater. "I'll be watching," he says, "I'm sure you'll do fine." I am far from sure, and I go backstage, where I see that there have been a number of cast changes that I didn't know about. There is only one person I recognize, a woman; I ask her if she has a copy of the script. She gives me a big thick book, and the dream fades, leaving a vague feeling of discomfort but far less so than when the dream began.

When I first woke up, I had no idea why I had dreamed such a thing, though clearly it was an anxiety dream (unprepared!). After I wrote the dream down and started to muse about it, it suddenly seemed very clear to me.

The role I was concerned about was not Hamlet but fatherhood, and this dream was a displacement of my fears about how well I'd do in this new role projected onto a classic anxiety dream backdrop.

My friend Jim was a fine college actor (which I was not), and I had worried aloud to my visiting friend that he seemed a better father than I thought I could be. Probably Jim was evoked by the associations of these other old college friends showing up, and my youthful envy at Jim's acting abilities somehow became a stand-in for my feelings that my friend might be a better father than I would be.

Why *Hamlet*? I had talked earlier in the week with someone about a recent Broadway production of *Hamlet* he had seen, and there had been a character dressed in Elizabethan garb on an episode of *ER* that I had watched that night. Hamlet was also notorious for indecision, and that's a trait I've often disliked in myself; I had even mentioned this to my friend as one of the things I worried about in regard to parenthood.

The woman who gave me the script might have been a stand-in for my wife, who always seems to me to be better prepared and calmer about life's ups and downs than I am. The script she handed me looked a great deal like the book *Your Baby and Your Child*, which someone had recently given us to help us prepare for parenthood and which my wife had been voraciously reading that night.

It seemed to me that this dream was telling me metaphorically that I was overly anxious about this upcoming change in my life, that I was letting my anxiety run away with me, and that although I might feel unprepared and was not, perhaps, as decisive as I might like, things were not totally out of control, especially because there were people in my life who would help and guide me.

This feeling emerged into my thoughts as I sat contemplating the dream. I did not say, "Aha! This equals that." Instead, I asked myself, what does the dream make me think of? What situation in my waking life does this dream put me in mind of?

I even quoted *Hamlet* correctly in my dream! It was a soliloquy I used to love and declaim when I was in college, a time in my life when I felt fairly self-confident, which may suggest that my unconscious was redirecting my attention to that sense of security (or it may have been simply one of those nonsense associations our unconscious makes in its narrative sweep).

The dream had nothing to do with college, but the association of my old friends with my new life situation seems to have evoked the setting and even the characters of the dream. Yet the dream was not about the past but about the future. My unconscious seems to have made use of images from my past, from the previous evening, and from random associations to offer me good advice, "You can do this if you allow yourself to feel confident about it."

As Jung observed, "The unconscious seems to be able to examine and draw conclusions from facts, much as consciousness does. It can even use certain facts and anticipate their possible results."

OK, so we are getting started here on a major task—trying to apply some simple, down-to-earth ideas to those elusive,

unopened letters from our unconscious. Now might be a good
time to look over your dream journal, if you're keeping one (and if
you're not, this would be a swell time to start). Some dreams seem
more obvious than others; find a fairly simple dream and try to
make some associations with it.

You can write, tape, word process, or even sketch these
associations.

What comes to mind first when you think about this dream? Is
there a central image or idea to this dream (like performance anxiety was in my dream, like being unable to move, trying to escape
danger, or whatever)?

What was in your thoughts the night before you had this
dream? What was going on in your day-to-day life?

Who is in this dream with you? What comes to mind when you
think of these people?

One thing you must remember is that being not-entirely-hon-
est about your relationships won't help. This activity is for you and
perhaps one or two people you trust; so, if your association to
someone who is supposed to be your friend is actually, "I don't
really like him though I act like I do," you have to say that rather
than the white lies we all tell sometimes about the people in our
lives!

Does the dream seem to be about how you feel about a situation, a person, an experience?

What does this person mean to you, really? What did this situation reveal to you about yourself or your friends?

Can you define, a little, what your feelings about the person or experience in the dream might be? Are they different from what you might say in your waking life?

Run your thoughts over the dream with these questions in front of you. Maybe something will pop into your head; maybe not.

If only a little—or nothing at all—pops out during this first stab, don't despair! There's more to come!

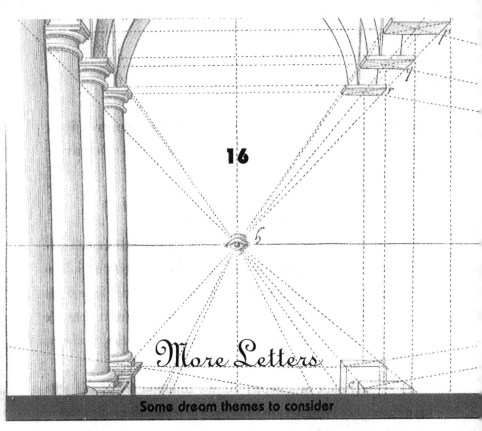

16

More Letters

Some dream themes to consider

The late John Gardner, a novelist very interested in myths and dreams, said that there were really only two plots in all of the world: "I went on a journey. . . ." and "A stranger came to town. . . ."

Well, there are more plots than this, but those two are among the best, and if you think about stories and movies you've liked, you'll probably recognize those two plots in many of them. Dreams are a bit like this, too. The details, the characters, the settings, and some of the plot lines even may vary wildly from individual to individual and from night to night. But the underlying images, ideas, and themes, so to speak, of our dreams can often be categorized fairly easily.

Dreams about the Past

Freud believed that all or most dreams were about childhood traumas, childhood sexuality, or wishes buried during childhood. Few contemporary dream theorists agree with this, but certainly some dreams replay childhood experiences—especially if our current life experience in some way touches upon earlier obstacles and hurts (or, for that matter, triumphs and joys).

As we said back in Chapter 10, it's common for people who have experienced disasters in their lives to replay those disasters in some form through their dreams. On a smaller scale, our unconscious seems always to be on the lookout for ways in which our current dilemmas mimic earlier ones. So, if your dreams often seem to recast you in childhood scenarios, you might want to consider in what ways your life today echoes or seems to repeat something from an earlier time.

Remember, though, that the unconscious works sometimes through symbolic substitution. As in this example:

"I had a dream about driving to the state of Georgia, which I realized later was about my mother, whose name is Georgia."

—Jennifer Cislo

———✦———

Dreams about Animals and Objects

Jung suggested that animals often represent an aspect of our own personality that we associate with that animal. Of course, we each have different responses to animals, so it's important to try and pinpoint how you feel about the cat, the wolf, or the bear in your dream.

Do you admire wolves or fear them? Do you melt when you see a cat, or would you prefer to kick it away? Does the animal remind you of any aspect of yourself?

Remember, too, that the English language is full of allusions to animals—have you behaved cattily lately? Do you feel that you are being treated like a dog? Have you been fierce like a lion? Put yourself in the place of the animal in your dream—does it connect to you in some deeper way?

"When I was fourteen, I had this dream about a frog. I loved that frog more than any single thing. He could fly. He was flying behind me, and some soldiers came and wanted to shoot the frog. Maybe the frog represented my feeling of being different, my imagination, my sense of myself as someone a little out of the ordinary."

—Michelle Tupko

Fritz Perls, the founder of gestalt therapy, believed that all elements in a dream, including objects, were part of the dreamer's personality. He suggested that the dreamer choose one of the less central objects in the dream, become that object, and act out that object's role in the dream in order to find out how it related to the dreamer.

You don't need to go quite that far to be aware that the objects in our dreams may represent some part of ourselves. Houses, rooms, and furniture for instance, are common dream symbols for our own minds, our unconscious, the different compartments of our personalities, the different ways we have furnished our lives. On the other hand, a chair in which you sit comfortably and feel supported is different from a chair that wobbles and feels unsteady.

Do any of the objects in your dream remind you of something in your waking life?

> "When I was dating this guy named Sean, I dreamed that he and I lived next door to each other. He came over to my house with his bag of laundry, smiled at me, and asked if I would do his laundry. I was taken by his smile and said I would, but my mom, who had been watching in the dream, became angry and demanded to know why I was doing Sean's laundry. This dream prompted me to review my relationship with Sean. He was always taking; I was always giving. The big load of dirty clothes he was offering me seemed very clear to me as a symbol of the whole relationship."
>
> —Anita Gill

———✳———

Character Dreams

The characters in our dreams whom we know may simply represent our actual feelings (or hidden fears or secret wishes) about important people in our lives. We may see our fathers behaving as we always wished they had or as we secretly feared they would. But familiar characters may also represent some aspect of that person that we see in ourselves.

A dream in which your boyfriend behaves like a pig toward you does not necessarily mean that he is a pig or even that you fear he's capable of piggish behavior—it may mean instead that some quality you don't like about him is something you've noticed in your own behavior. The dream may be pointing out to you that you're capable of being equally swinish.

This is called "projection," and we all do it, both in waking life and in our dreams, projecting our darker qualities onto someone else.

If your dreams frequently feature a familiar character behaving badly, this may be what Jung referred to as a "shadow," a dream figure who embodies the aspects of our personalities that we have disowned, but which our unconscious may be telling us we need to recognize and come to terms with. Jungian analyst Marie-Louise von Franz points out, "The shadow becomes hostile only when he is ignored or misunderstood."

"All dreams point out to the individual the unique meaning of his or her unique life."
—Marie-Louise von Franz

But what about characters we don't know who turn up in our dreams? Some may be stand-ins for people in our real life or people we have complicated feelings about, who we may not be able to fully accept, even in our dreams.

Or these characters may represent some part of ourselves with which we are struggling and about which we are unsure.

> "I once had a dream about a little boy who was abandoned. He was about eleven years old, and it was my responsibility to take care of him. I just appeared in front of him, and knew what to do. I wanted to dedicate my entire life to him. I woke up feeling like a different person. I think this dream had a lot to do with holding onto a sense of innocence and wonder."
>
> —Dodd Bates

— ✦ —

Dreams about the Opposite Sex

Since a tremendous amount of our time and energy is spent in trying to get the attention, love, and desire of the opposite sex, it would be odd indeed if these themes did not reverberate in our dreams, too. Erotic dreams are common throughout life, though probably never as common as they are in adolescence (but you knew that). Sometimes, an erotic dream may be as simple as a wish fulfillment or a gentle hint from your unconscious that your feelings for someone may be stronger than you've thought:

> "Every time I have an erotic dream about someone, I end up getting involved with him."
> —Sarah Kendzior

But sex can be a metaphor just like anything else. Sexual dreams can be about wanting to be desired by someone particular or wanting to be desirable in general, with a particular face and body attached through associations. They can be about fear of desire, fear of rejection, or fear of being betrayed. They can be about a desire to be in control or a fear of being out of control in new situations. They can be about learning how to come to terms with new desires and new sensations.

> "The mind is a complicated sex machine! I think the psyche uses sexual dreams to focus our attention on important issues. I had a sexual dream about a man I'd never seen before, which was a very positive experience. As I was

about to walk out the door and wake up, four voices said, 'No, you cannot leave. There is important energy here!' And I'm like, 'Oh, OK,' and I just hung out there for a while. And it was true; there was this very positive energy there for me. It seems to me the dream was about how I could use sexual energy as a positive force in life."

—Adriane Vawter

But of course not all dreams about the opposite sex are sexual dreams. In fact, they may not be about others at all, but about us. Jung speaks of the *anima* and *animus*, the female side of the male psyche and the male side of the female psyche, respectively. Sometimes, in our dreams, idealized or even repulsive male and female figures may represent a buried part of ourselves we need to accept and explore. If we don't, Jung believed, we go on projecting onto real men and women the ideal (or repulsive) image we carry around in our heads.

"I had this recurring dream about a girl, someone I'd never met but knew I would meet eventually. I knew everything about her—her hair color, her smile, the kind of music she liked, the way she carried her knapsack. I kept looking for that girl in every girl I'd meet, only the girls never measured up, and it really depressed me. Then, I realized she was just this dream image, and I can't spend my life looking for some impossible angel!"

—Billy Maitland

Dreams about Conflict and Death

Many dreams have some kind of conflict within them, just as our real lives are filled with disagreements, minor battles, and major strivings. Conflicts with our families, with our loved ones, at school or work, conflicts within ourselves—all of these are refracted through the lens of our dreams.

Dream theorist Calvin Hall says that many conflicts presented in our dreams, regardless of their setting, seem to go back to an initial conflict, ". . . the conceptual struggle that a child goes through in trying to define his feelings toward his mother and father and their feelings toward him."

This conflict, which you doubtless know only too well, may ebb and flow throughout our lives. Also, it touches upon issues of freedom and who's-in-charge-here and is often not entirely resolved, even long after we have left home and established our independence. In our dreams, this conflict may take many guises but always seems especially urgent and often life-threatening, because how we view ourselves in relationship to our parents is crucial in forming our own self-image.

> "For a while, when my parents were getting divorced, I had this series of dreams. They would be ordinary, boring dreams. I'd be walking through the house or sitting and reading, and then someone would come in and try to kill me. I wouldn't recognize the person. They didn't look anything like my parents, and they'd always be different, too, but I always knew it was about my parents and that the person was trying to kill me. I would try to fight them or try to escape, but I would always get killed. Finally—and I think this was when I decided that the whole divorce thing wasn't my problem and I wasn't going to let it destroy me—I got up and left one of these dreams—just walked out, as if to say, 'You can't kill me,' and I never had a dream like that again."
>
> —Karen Garrity

Dreams of death are probably subject to as much misunderstanding, superstition, and downright silliness as sex dreams. If you dream that someone you love is dead, that doesn't mean you wish them dead in any real sense. But let's face it, there are times in our lives when we secretly resent someone we love so much that we might briefly wish them out of our lives. Dreams can certainly reflect this kind of secret, guilty wish. Yet we're not really guilty of anything except being human. Similarly, most of us have had a dream in which we are trying to kill someone or are being threatened by someone whom we care deeply about in waking life. This does not mean you actually wish to kill your aunt or have reason to fear your significant other.

It may suggest that some aspect of the relationship is in danger and needs attending to or that you are afraid of losing an important person from your life. It may suggest that the part of yourself that this person represents to you is, in some sense, dying.

But not all death dreams are sad. Just as in a forest, where old trees must die so new ones can grow, old relationships and friendships and attachments sometimes have to die before new ones can bud.

"I was standing in my backyard with my cousin Grace and

was surrounded by my entire family. In my hand I held my cordless telephone. I picked it up, and someone said, 'He's dead.' I repeated this to Grace, and she began to scream. Suddenly, I was in my godmother's yard (next door), and my family was inside her house, mourning. I stood inside the wooden clubhouse Mike and Grace and I had built when we were younger, peeking out of the window, afraid to really look. In the distance, I could see Mike, in a coffin, standing upright, facing me.

"I was not really frightened by this dream so much as saddened. It seems to me it's about our childhood memories and the closeness that just isn't there any more but that I know had to die in order for me to grow up, leave home, find out about the world."

—Alexandra Krakow

Dreaming that you have died can be alarming, certainly, but does not in any way imply that you are terminally ill, being stalked, or need to purchase an assault weapon. It may mean that what Jung calls your "persona," the mask that you present to the outside world, isn't working for you any more and needs reassessment. It may mean that an old you is being cast aside so that a new you can take its place. It may mean that you are under a lot of stress and fear that some part of yourself is dying or that a major life transition is imminent, with all the anxieties that that can evoke.

Since death looms throughout our lives as the ultimate loss, it is not surprising that smaller losses should be symbolized through death in our unconscious or that images associated with mortality should resound through our dreamworld.

Dreaming about someone who has already died can be equally eerie, but often such dreams are not dark and fearful but strangely moving. They seem to suggest that the emotions and energy we associated with that person are not gone but live on in our psyche; these dreams may even contain messages of renewal and hope.

"Several months after my friend died from cancer, I had a dream at about four in the morning. In the dream, it was also four in the morning; Karen came to me as a spirit. She counseled me not to take the shortcut in life but to travel the long way around (I'm not sure what that means!). She was about to float out the window, and I begged her to stay, saying there was so much that had happened since she died that I wanted to tell her. She put her hand on mine and said, 'You don't have to, because I am always with you.'"

—Jennifer Cislo

First Dream It—Then Do It

Medard Boss, a Swiss dream theorist, said, "We cannot consider dreaming and waking as two entirely different spheres. . . . It is always the identical human being who awakens from his dreams and who maintains his identity throughout all his waking and dreaming."

So, as you think about your dreams, think about your waking life, too. As you start to work on mining this rich lode of dream images, it might be useful to make a list of some of the important people in your waking life. Do your dreams include any of these people? Do the strangers in your dreams remind you of any of these people? Do they remind you of yourself?

Write (or draw) a sort of brief self-sketch. How do you see yourself? What gives you pleasure in your life? What (or whom) do you see as casting a shadow on your life? What kinds of choices are you having to make in your life? Are there some decisions you're having a hard time making? Are there parts of your life you'd like to see change?

What is getting in your way right now? Do any of your dreams seem to echo these concerns?

What is the emotional content of your dreams?

> "I often understand my dreams by considering the emotions in them. Am I detached? Angry? Sad? What's making me feel this way? Is it like anything in my life?"
>
> —Heather Bogan

Remember, too, as you slog through some of this rather challenging stuff, that your dreams are not criticizing you—or patting you on the back. Dreams are neither moral nor immoral; they just are. They are not necessarily telling you that something is good, or wrong, or needs to be changed. They are merely road maps of your unconscious. But if you follow them, they may take you to unexpected places.

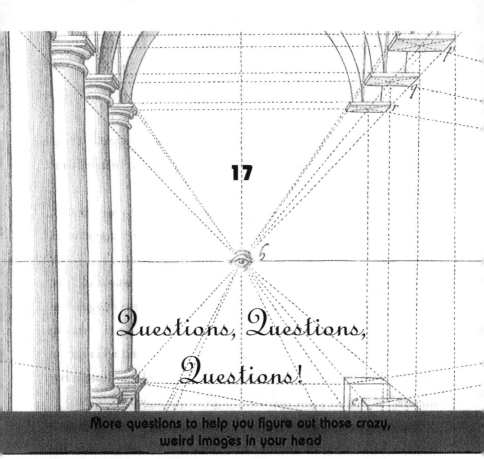

17

Questions, Questions, Questions!

More questions to help you figure out those crazy, weird images in your head

In his book *A Little Course on Dreams*, Robert Bosnak says that his first response upon listening to someone's dream is usually, "I haven't the faintest idea what this is all about."

Does this sound familiar?

Do your dreams seem too crazy to try and make sense of them? Freud says, "Dreams are often most profound when they seem most crazy."

Do your dreams seem too trivial or too silly to bother with?

Bosnak says, "Resistances often make a dream seem trivial at first glance; after some mining work, these apparently insignificant dreams often yield a lot of material."

Would you rather just appreciate the weirdness of your dreams, maybe make creative use of them, instead of fretting about what they mean?

You're in good company! I often feel the same way and have probably spent far more energy trying to mold dream images into something than trying to yank something out of them. And in Chapter 18, we'll talk about dreams and creativity and what dream expert Montague Ullman refers to as the need to "honor our dreams" as well as scour them for clues to our inner conflicts.

But most people who flirt with the fascinating world of dreams want at some time or another to plunge a little deeper into the interpretive mode. So, even if your eyes glaze over right now at the thought of trying to decipher the meaning of that giant red bagel, that weirdo who lives next door, that pit of piranhas who all looked like your ex-boyfriend, . . . at some point, you might wish to come back to those images and look at them with fresh eyes.

So, if you skimmed over the last two chapters, that's OK; they will still be there on the day you decide you want to dig a little deeper.

And when that day (or night) comes, there are a few more questions to ask yourself.

What does the dream feel like?

Dr. Eugene Gendlin, a dream theorist from the University of Chicago, suggests that dreamers consider what he calls the "felt sense" of the dream, the way their bodies felt in the dream, or the way their bodies feel when they recall the dream. Since dreams often deal with peculiar physical sensations (pounding heart, paralyzed limbs), recalling the physicality of the dream may give you some ideas about the message of the dream.

What is the setting of the dream? What does it remind you of?

The place you dream about may be familiar yet somehow not quite right—your house but not your house, your high school yet much, much bigger. How does the setting make you feel? How does the way the setting looked relate to the way the place actually is? What other places in your

> " . . . *It is dreams*
> *That lift us to the flow-*
> *ing, changing world.*"
> —*William Butler Yeats*

life does the setting remind you of? If it is an unfamiliar setting (the planet Venus, a mysterious street corner), what about it stands out? Is it like any place you've ever been? Does it have a particular atmosphere (Warm? Creepy? Full of light? Crisscrossed with shadows?)? Does the atmosphere of this place evoke any associations?

What is the plot of the dream?

Does the story as you recall it remind you of anything in your current life? Is there a choice or decision implied in the dream? Does the dream retell something that actually happened to you, only in a different way? What are the differences? Does the plot seem implausible to you? What are the absurd parts? Do they remind you of anything in your real life that may also seem absurd or ridiculous?

What are the objects like in your dream?

Are any objects unusual in color, size, or shape? Do they make you think of anything else? Are there objects that are used in a way other than their ordinary use? Does any object seem especially important in the dream? What is your association with that object? What is that object used for in waking life? What else could it be used for? What else does it resemble?

What are the relationships like in the dream?

Do people behave badly toward each other? Does someone behave badly toward you? Do you behave badly toward someone? Does it remind you of anything in your real life? Who were you with the day before the dream occurred? Who were you thinking about? Is there someone you wished you were with recently instead of the people you were with? Is there someone you wish was no longer part of your life at the moment? Is there someone in the dream who reminds you of yourself? Of some part of yourself? What part?

What past memory does the dream remind you of?

What were you like then? What is different about your life now? Who are you trying to be in your life? Where would you like to go in your life? Is there anything in the dream that seems to echo these concerns?

How does the dream end?

Does the dream leave you feeling uneasy? Unsatisfied? Can you imagine a better ending for the dream? What would happen if you allowed yourself to reenter the dream and go on with the story? Where might it take you?

What is the residue of the dream?

What position was your body in when you woke up? Do any fragments of a song, memories of a color, shreds of a conversation, or random words linger from the dream? What was your first thought after you remembered the dream? What five words could you quickly say that would help describe the dream for someone else? What part of the dream most puzzles you? Why? What immediately comes to mind when you think about this puzzling part of the dream? What most frustrates you about your own life? Is the puzzling part of the dream in any way like the frustrating parts of your life?

We've dwelt a great deal in the past few chapters on the darker side of dream imagery, haven't we?

Well, sure, the dreams most of us find puzzling and which move us toward wanting to understand them tend to be the dreams that are troubling, complex, and dark.

But the dark side of dreams coexists with the joyful side. Dream researcher Ann Faraday says, "The only correct interpretation of a dream is one that gives the dreamer a joyful 'Aha!' experience of insight."

Light comes after dark, joy often follows sorrow or fear, and insight often follows utter confusion. Dreams tell us this, perhaps more surely even than life does.

18

The Little People Made Me Do It!

Dreams can renew and enhance your creative instincts; your dreams can inspire your writing, drawing, dancing, singing, and more

OK, so we've heard dreams called meaningful and pointless, prophetic and a waste of time, and full of both dark intimations about sexual desire and uplifting images of spiritual longing.

We've been told that dreams may be nothing more than the result of neurochemicals coursing through the cerebral cortex, that they might contain vestiges of an alternate channel of communication, and that they can offer us solace and insight—and throat-wrenching terror.

Is that all? No! Dreams can provide fresh perspective and new ideas, they can inspire poems and paintings, and they can infuse novels and films.

The great poets William Blake and William Butler Yeats sought to capture their dreams through their often mystical poetry. Novelists as diverse as the urbane Graham Greene and the acerbic William S. Burroughs have utilized their dreams in their work—and even published their dream journals.

Salvador Dali's eerie dream paintings (melting clocks, rain inside taxi cabs) have become world famous, as have the enigmatic dream portraits of René Magritte (little men in bowler hats with apples or fish for heads). The contemporary artist Jasper Johns dreamed of painting the American flag—and did so in real life, creating an immensely powerful and influential series of paintings about modern America.

Filmmakers from the witty Spanish surrealist Luis Bunuel to the multitalented Orson Welles have based films on the strange cinematic images projected in the theater of their unconscious.

Dreams have also helped to find missing objects, to solve personal dilemmas, to discover a chemical secret, to invent a simple household tool, and even to win the Nobel Prize!

Scholars might argue about the ultimate meaning of dreams,

but few would dispute that dreams, however they come about and whatever they might actually say about the nature of the mind, can truly renew and enhance the creative instinct.

Take that chemical secret I mentioned. Friedrich Kekule was a professor of chemistry at the University of Ghent, in Belgium. He had been trying to solve the structural puzzle of the benzene molecule. One night, in 1865, he fell asleep and began to dream of atoms dancing before him, forming patterns.

Kekule's dream atoms formed snakes and began to twist and writhe. Suddenly, one of the snakes seized its own tail, whirling around and around in a circle.

Kekule leaped awake. He began to scribble down what he had seen, trying to work out the meaning of the dream. Based on his dream image of a snake devouring its own tail, he constructed a model of a closed molecular ring with an atom of carbon and hydrogen at each point of a hexagon—a discovery that helped revolutionize organic chemistry.

Kekule didn't worry about whether his dream was too weird, was about sex, or contained an archetype from the collective unconscious. He instantly saw a vital connection between his dream and his daytime preoccupations and used the dream in a practical manner to fuel the engine of his creativity.

Years later, in presenting a paper about this discovery to a skeptical audience of his peers, he said, "Let us learn to dream, gentlemen, and then perhaps we may find the truth."

There are dozens of similar anecdotes, some even stranger. Elias Howe, a nineteenth-century American inventor, dreamed the design for the first sewing machine. Frederick Banting, a Canadian physician, dreamed about the pancreas of a dog (I'm not making this up!), which helped lead Banting and his colleagues to isolate insulin in nonhuman sources, saving the lives of millions of diabetics.

Otto Loewi, a German physiologist, dreamed about experiments on frogs' hearts (no, really), dreams that helped him prove a theory about the chemical transmission of nervous impulses; Loewi won the Nobel Prize for Medicine for those theories in 1936.

On a smaller (and somewhat less bizarre) scale, dreams have been used by people much like you to solve problems and inspire a creative approach to thinking about life.

"When I can't find something, like an old journal or a letter, I will ask to remember it in a dream. Not always but surprisingly often, I will see the place it's hidden in my dream that night. It's like my unconscious sees things better than my conscious mind does!"

—Carey Edlund

"During exams in college, I can often visualize what the test will be like in my dreams, which is helpful sometimes and unnerving other times. When I've been in plays, I dream I'm on stage rehearsing my lines—and I feel more prepared, and more confident that way."

—Glenn Williams

"Once, I asked for a dream that would help me decide which of two men to choose. I dreamed I was in my apartment, where I introduced the two men and sat them on chairs in opposite corners of the room. Just then, a hurricane developed, heading straight for my apartment. I ran to hold onto one of the men, and then turned to run and hold onto the other. Finally, I judged that the safest thing to do was grab hold of the empty couch. The hurricane hit, and I found myself swimming up a river with the two men hanging on my arms. I knew I would drown if I did not get them off me. I pushed them away and swam up the river— I guess the answer the dream gave me is pretty clear!"

—Jennifer Cislo

"I've used dreams to create sculptures—really trying to make a piece of wood or metal look like the twisted things in my dreams. And for a while, I was in a band, and I dreamed a whole song. I mean, the song wasn't in my head before the dream, and then it was playing over and over in the background of the dream. When I woke up, I still remembered it and I wrote it down."

—Billy Maitland

Based on hundreds of years of anecdotal evidence, it appears that dreams really can help to create new ideas, nudge aside mental roadblocks, and even allow whole works of art to spring from our heads like Athena springing from the forehead of Zeus.

How do dreams do such things?

Does paying attention to our dreams open up some valve, allowing creativity to flow more freely? Or are dreams simply so rich in possibility and in juxtaposing ideas that they stimulate our thoughts?

If you've read this far, you won't be surprised to learn that . . . we don't know the answer. It is clear that dreams provide problem-solving insight and inspiration for many people. How and why they do so, like so many other areas of dream research, remains murky.

But sleep and dreams have been linked over and over to the immensely complex brain waves we call "thoughts." Many studies show that when we are deprived of REM sleep, our thoughts are slower and we are less focused and less likely to solve problems. One recent study showed that students who got more REM sleep than normal scored significantly higher in an intensive language course than did students who did not increase their REM sleep levels.

So, perhaps REM sleep and its attendant dream state nourish consciousness. Perhaps the entire process of dreaming is ultimately a kind of refueling for our overactive minds. Perhaps dreams are brain food.

Or are they more like elves?

Creative people have often claimed that their inspirational dreams seemed almost to come from some other source altogether, much the way ancient people believed dreams were the whispered voices of gods and demons.

The eighteenth-century Italian composer Giuseppe Tartini dreamed that the devil played an extraordinary violin sonata for him, which became Tartini's most famous piece "The Devil's Sonata."

Did the devil give Tartini his tune?

The poet William Blake, who was also a wonderful artist, dreamed that his dead brother Robert visited him and showed him a new method of copper engraving, which completely changed Blake's style. Was Blake's dream visitor a spirit, as he believed?

The famous nineteenth-century British author Robert Louis Stevenson referred to his best stories as the work of "little people," who wrote them while he slept—like in the fairy tale of the shoe-maker and the elves. He credited these dream friends with telling him better stories while he slept than any he could tell on his own while awake.

Most famously, Stevenson's little people provided him with a crucial scene and the dark, urgent theme for *The Strange Case of Dr. Jekyll and Mr. Hyde.*

Did Stevenson really believe that tiny elves were working away in his brain, weaving tales? No. He was a strange man, but not a lunatic. In a memoir, he wonders about these dream assistants asking, "Who are they, then? And who is the dreamer?" Stevenson's idea—and his question—touches upon something we have heard, in many ways, in many voices, throughout this book: How do we separate the dreamer from the dream? How does our inner self connect to the one we present to the world?

Certainly, our dreaming mind works in different ways than does our conscious mind. Dreams are, perhaps, more like ghostly visitors or elves than like ourselves, for they are elusive, come out mostly at night, and are liable to vanish if we look at them too hard.

Like Blake's visitor, Tartini's devil, and Stevenson's little people, dreams peek out from a part of the self that is half hidden. As such, they are not bound by the world of logic and propriety; they are free to be the tricksters, jugglers, clowns, and poets of the psyche, visitors indeed from the infinite world of our unconscious.

Havelock Ellis, the pioneering British psychologist said, "The infinite can only be that which stretches far beyond the boundaries of our own personality. It is the charm of dreams that they introduce us into a new infinity. We are joyfully borne up in the air in the arms of angels."

The work of elves, visitors, tricksters, poets, angels—this view of dreams isn't so different from the Native American idea of dream guides we talked about way back in Chapter 4!

In my own experience, dreams have guided me to plots, characters, and even details for stories and plays. The first play I wrote was based on a dream—two dwarves sitting in a closet playing a peculiar game of cards. "Who were they," I wondered, "and what were they doing there?" So, I wrote a play about it.

Around the same time, I had a series of dreams about my uncle the magician (I have no uncle who is a magician) and my search for him. I also had recurring dreams about broken glasses, broken mirrors, and broken cups. I used all these images for a short story about a foolish young man's quest for a mythical uncle.

When I first began teaching, I had a huge, largely uninterested class. I wanted to find a way to get them writing and to get them to see writing as something useful in their lives. I had a dream about a giant, white bear. When I awoke, I remembered a fairy tale I had loved as a child, *East of the Sun and West of the Moon*, which features a giant, white bear.

I looked it up and used it as a teaching story about the quest for self-understanding, for taking control of our lives, for making good our mistakes, and for remaining true to ourselves.

The story clicked with these reluctant students, and I subsequently used it in other writing classes; then I turned it into the libretto for an opera for young people and a play as well.

It was one of the most successful ideas I ever had—and I owe it all to the dream of the white bear.

More recently, I was asked to write a play for teenaged actors at the Center for Creative Youth, at Wesleyan University. I didn't have an idea in my head, but one morning I woke up with the lingering fragment of a dream—a girl with a frightened face, as if *she* had just awakened from a bad dream. I found myself murmuring, "Anna's Dream," though I did not then know anyone named Anna.

I didn't recall any more of the dream, but the face and that title stuck with me, and I ended up calling my play "Anna's Dream." It won a prize.

I'm not telling you all this to impress you (you'd have to be pretty easily impressed) but to say that dream inspirations don't have to make sense (dwarves in a closet?), emerge fully developed (a giant, white bear?), or even be fully remembered (a frightened face?) to exert creative power over your life.

I've had plenty of other dream ideas that went nowhere, and most of my writing is not derived from my dreams. But I feel a strange connection to the stories and plays that did grow from my dreams, as if they were more deeply mine than some of my other work.

Because I'm a writer my dreams become writing, but your dreams can become drawings, dances, sculptures, or songs just as easily.

How? Here are some suggestions:

1. *Look for the images that surprise, amuse, or enchant you.*

Remember that when you are considering creative work, you are not seeking to understand the dream so much as to harness it. The images need not be from the same dream—you are still the same dreamer, after all! Scan your dream log quickly (those titles might come in handy here!) for the fragments that most intrigue you, that seem to call out for something more.

2. *Don't fret about coherence.*

You are looking for material, not completion. You are looking for a jumping-off point, not a finished project. Find dream material that moves you in some way, and see where it takes you.

3. *Don't work on the image; let the image work on you.*

If you are a writer, write down everything that comes to mind when you contemplate the enormous dream streetlight, the fog-bound street. If you are a dancer, try to move as you moved in the dream; try to move as the dream makes you feel in memory. If you play an instrument, sit in a dark room with your violin or your clarinet and try to hear what the dream sounded like. Try to play the feeling of the dream.

If you are a photographer, try to take photographs of people, objects, or places that in some way resemble your dream photos, or which might allow someone a peek into the gallery of your dreamworld. If you draw, put some strange music on and try to draw everything that comes to mind when you think of the dream. Don't force it; try to let the story/poem/song/picture grow, as if it were a part of nature.

4. *Don't be bound by the dream.*

If your story seems to veer off from the original dream image, let it veer. If the painting based on your dream ends up looking more like a self-portrait, paint on! If the melody requires more notes or the screenplay needs more characters, don't fret about being unfaithful to the dream. This is not therapy, nor is it about setting an idea in stone—it's about freeing your creative impulses. So, if the dream leads you away from the initial image, follow, follow!

5. *Respect the irrational.*

One of the most creatively fertile aspects of dreams is

their startling ability to turn things upside down, to *not* emulate reality. Personally, I hate stories that end "and then I woke up." I'd rather wonder, as in a story by Franz Kafka or Gabriel Garcia Marquez, whether the events are meant to be understood as fantastic or realistic. One of the endearing qualities of Magritte's dream paintings is that they do not announce that they are dreams—they're just strange, funny, off-the-wall paintings (e.g., a railroad train steaming out of a fireplace, for instance, a man looking through a window at a man looking through a window at a man looking through a window). Absurdity is not limited to the dreamworld, certainly, and showing us how the preposterous coexists with the mundane is one of the lessons—and the pleasures—of dream creativity.

6. *Dreams are not art critics—don't be intimidated.*

You don't have to be a polished poet to try to capture a dream in poetry; you don't have to have ever taken a sculpture class to try and make concrete that dream figure that haunts you. You don't have to be a film student to try to create an exciting screenplay based on the bizarre chase scene in your nightmares. The whole idea of dream creativity is to take the leap, as if you were still in that dreamworld and could do anything, anything you desire.

7. *But don't expect miracles.*

Of course, just because you hear a magical melody in your dream doesn't mean you will be able to play that tune on a piano—especially if you've never played the piano before. You may even find it frustrating trying to capture that perfect image from your unconscious on paper—welcome to the club! Dreams are no guarantee of artistic success; they are instead invitations to participate in a realm outside our day-to-day preoccupations, to join in a modern version of a truly ancient dance.

So what are you waiting for?

In the next few pages, I've reproduced some brief poems and stories based on dreams to give you a quick glance at how your dreams can feed your creative writing. Read them and then try it yourself. Remember, creativity isn't about the product; it's about the process. You may not come up with anything that you like at first, but as with any new exercise, you can get good at it if you keep pushing—and keep dreaming!

The process of falling asleep and dreaming is itself an intriguing area to explore creatively. We all know how strange the border between waking and sleep can feel—why not try to capture it in words (or in colors or in sounds)? In this first poem, the author compares the time before we fall asleep to the calm before a storm, a time when senses are heightened and the universe seems more alive.

> *rising storm catches dream*
> *sitting alone*
> *in wet buggy night*
> *watching the cat-eye moon*
> *cast shadows of haze*
> *upon the grass in my yard.*
> *i see fog ghosts arise*
> *and dance high above the trees*
> *while winds part lips*

(and whisper)
about the coming
of the storm
and drifting between sleep
head heavy like rocks catching waves.
i listen
to the buzz of mosquito bodies
(turning to dust)
and the splash of the sprinkler
washing them away.
　　　　—Amy Garbo

———✦———

The act of remembering dreams—or trying to remember them, failing to remember them, or feeling like that dream memory is just on the tip of your mind—is also a useful subject for poetic exploration. Famous dead authors like Edgar Allan Poe and Samuel Taylor Coleridge are celebrated for poems that seek to recapture the elusive romance of dream life. But you don't have to be famous (or dead) to try it yourself.

In this piece, the poet conjures up a lost world that is personal yet contains some familiar dream archetypes as well.

Droplet

I had forgotten about you,
the joys you bestowed,
the precious hours we spent together.
when I was alone
I forgot all of my dreams
when I dived into those painted pictures
vividly drawn in my head.
Take me back again, I beg,
steal me to that land
where trees are black, the sky green
and red rivers flood their banks.
Let us ride that white horse of feathers,
let us fly the unreachable clouds.
Let me fall asleep amongst
yellow tulips on blue sand.
I will close my eyes and restore
that blanket that transformed
into a shining white angel
with hair of gold.
Untouched by day, a knight by night
you will absorb my soul.

Drowned and without body I'll float
now I am light as a droplet.
I can see my rusted green fairies
with their light pink hair.
I can feel my silken robe
liquifying with the air.
The castle covered with ferns now stands,
her gates open to me.
She will sing Ovid's poetry
while I travel her hands.
I am asleep on the bed below,
his velvet surrounds shivering souls.
I bathe in a lake of silver tears
and with creatures unseen, unknown,
eat grapes on her soft lavender shore.
The fairies dance farewell
when you come down from your clouds.
And I sleep last time amongst soft grass,
last time breathing your breath.

—Pelin Batu

———✦———

The next writer often uses her dreams in writing poetry, though the poems are not necessarily about the dreams themselves but about images and ideas and ways of looking at the world that her dreams help clarify for her.

In "Feverish," the poet has taken several dream images (mermaids, a dog, an angry father) from different moments in her life and woven them into an hallucinatory poem.

Feverish

In third grade
I used to draw pictures
of beautiful mermaids with
huge sparkling tails
but I lived on land
in my backyard, in the city.
My teacher said
that they lived in water
where they could swim free
and I told him no,
that sometimes they get tired.
Sometimes,
when the night is dark

and the sea is deep,
deep blue
mermaids crawl out onto
land, flipping
their emerald tails
against the beach.
They slither out of the water
because they cannot bear
to swim anymore.
They tire of being mermaids.
My teacher told me
whales do the same thing
fling themselves onto
the sand.
He said they died
when they did that.
Dogs sense anger.
When the room
is filled with screaming,
they curl up with their
tails and whimper sympathetically.
My father explained that to me

and while he was smoking
at the kitchen table
I started to argue
about the dog's sixth sense.
We fought
and he stood up with his hands
on the back of the chair.
The dog barked and jumped
at the window
aching to get out.
A bulging vein
in your forehead
crawling right up the middle
means you are a genius.
If you lean up close to someone
and feel the blood
running through the
smooth frontal skin
it should be considered
very carefully
and reverently.

Yesterday
you held me
up, off the floor
so that my wet tail
did not scrape against
the cracking tile,
You said you were going
to carry me back to sea.
And for a second
my cheek was close
to your forehead.
I was afraid that vein
would burst.
You were wonderful, wanting
to help me live
but I guess you haven't heard
about mermaids' passion
for resting their bodies
on land.
You pleaded that I go back with you
to the fresh blue ocean.

While I slowly breathed air
never meant for me,
my dog whimpered at your kindness.
　　　—Michelle Tupko

—— ✦ ——

About the following poem, the author recalls, "I went into New York and saw this exhibit of Edward Hopper paintings. They were really bleak and powerful, with all these amazing faces. That night, I dreamed about the paintings, and the dream became this poem."

When Edward Spoke

"I'm tired,"
he said.
"These women are killing me.
Let me tell you."
The one who will not look
up from her cup of tea;
whose hat is a morose frown
on her small head,
drooping down over her thoughts
like a rainbow over

a forsaken child.
The one who turns
away from her lover
while he thrashes to sleep;
who dresses too quickly after
making love—afraid of
the moonlight
and the tender curves of her
arms that may again
reach out for him.
And more than anything
the one who will not turn
her head, whose face
is never known;
whose hands are folded
just so, keeping her breasts
a perfect secret.
The one who will not turn her head;
whose attention is not for me
whose lips are smeared
with the rouge of loneliness.
And when you enter

this city you can see the shadow
of a tunnel,
the side of buildings.
But these women
you cannot imagine,
do not even remember
until you are peeking
through a glass window
at suppertime.
Your own wife cooking at home
waiting for you to return
And you are lost here.
"I am so happy,"
he said,
"that everyone else seems
sad to me.
But at night I am alone.
There is silence.
There is stillness.
And I murmur to myself
that the moon is like a mad woman
rising from her tomb

searching to find lovers
as I am searching to forget lovers.
It is then I am afraid
that I have never been happy,
rather so miserable
that I have misplaced my joy."
And he switched off the light.
—Michelle Tupko

———✦———

The following two stories came directly out of dreams. In "Red," the author shows us what a dream looks like from the inside—that feeling of disjointedness, eerie familiarity, and ominous possibility that dreams so often present to us.

Red

The phone rings violently, awakening me from my sleep. The voice at the other end asks, "Are you awake?"

"Yes," I say in my usual raspy morning voice. The mucus at the back of my throat slowly slides down into that infinite nowhere.

"Well, get up, then! It's already seven o'clock!"

So, I begin my usual routine. I am too tired to actually get up from my blissfully warm, inviting bed. But I am a light sleeper; I will not be able to go back to sleep. So I light a cigarette and turn on the TV.

"Good day, New York! It's 7:10, and today, the weather will be rainy in the low forties. . . . " Julie Golden says as I stare into the TV. The hot smoke of my cigarette forms a nasty film inside my mouth. I can taste the rank odor of my mouth. I can no longer stand it. I finally get up from my only form of pleasure and walk toward the bathroom.

The apartment is so dim, always dim. I hate it. I'm still in a daze as I blindly search for the light switch. I walk toward the sink and turn the hot water on. "Damn it! It's hot!" I shout, as I quickly pull my hand from underneath the running faucet.

I turn on the cold water, cup my hands, gather some water, and clean all the sleepies from my face.

I look up. I see myself in the mirror. "It's going to be a long day," I think, as I see the bloodshot eyes staring back at me. I slowly begin to inspect my face. "How the hell can I get rid of these bags?" I think to myself, as I stretch the skin on my face.

I laugh. I'm reminded of something. My face reminds me of someone, someone I saw with the skin stretched out like that. I cannot remember who or where. So I just laugh, as I walk into my steaming shower.

As usual, I waste time in the shower, cleaning every possible crevice of my body over and over again. I have wasted an hour; now it's 8:05. "Why do you always do this?" I shout, as I rush from the shower. I still have to make my bed, because if I don't Mom will freak (she treats me like a five-year-old!). I have to get dressed and take my vitamins, and I still have to read that stupid music book. And I can't forget my usual make-up regimen—I have to look presentable in case I meet my soul mate.

I finish all this forty minutes later. I now have ten minutes to get to class.

"I really have to get my act together," I think, as I lock the door to my apartment.

I rush down Ninth Avenue. Drops of rain soak my recently butchered hair. I am reviewing the limited list of irregular verbs I have managed to memorize for today's Italian quiz, when I remember something—I forgot to bring that damn music book with me!

Suddenly, a loud honk pierces my left ear. What is all this noise about? I turn, and my brown eyes dilate. I am standing an inch from the hood of a cab. I am just standing there, stopped, in the middle of Ninth Avenue!

I jerk back and forth stupidly, my hands trembling in my coat pockets. Reason finally takes over and I slowly move toward the corner of Ninth and Forty-fifth. "Hey! Watch where you're going!" the cab driver shouts at me. I feel my cheeks and ears turn red, and all I can do is lower my head in embarrassment.

As I'm descending the stairs to the subway, I realize what has happened. "You could have died," these are the only words running through my head. My stomach contracts, my legs begin to shake uncontrollably and my hands are like two blocks of ice. My head feels like it's burning up. I look down at my body—tiny red spots cover my entire chest.

I try to swallow, but I cannot. The complete culmination of all I am feeling rolls down my cheek in one tiny tear. I wipe the tear from my cheek, take a deep breath, and wait for the train to arrive. I look at my watch; I am already two minutes late for Italian.

Five minutes later, the train pulls into the station. I take a seat behind a man wearing a dark blue suit and an older woman who reminds me of my grandmother. There are lots of little kids on the train, and a woman is towering over this mob of children, trying to control them. I stare at these children for some time because they remind me so much of my brother and sister.

One child captivates me; her beautiful red hair is hypnotizing. She slowly brushes aside a curl that has delicately fallen onto her face. Her hair is deep red, like fire. I have never seen anything like it. She stares back at me and smiles.

Our stares are interrupted by the incomprehensible, staticky voice of the conductor. It seems we have reached our destination, so I stand and walk toward the sliding doors. The doors do not open.

A bright light rips through the front window. I walk to the window and notice that brick by brick, the wall of the tunnel is falling apart. As the train slowly moves into the light, my heart begins to pound, and my knees weaken.

I turn and see that every single child is quietly seated. They are no longer shrieking but patiently sitting, as if waiting for something to happen.

I shout at their teacher, "What is going on?"

The light becomes brighter, so bright it's hard to decipher anyone on the train. I collapse in complete exhaustion.

Slowly, I come to. "Miss, miss, are you all right?" the man with the dark blue suit asks me.

I cannot answer. I try to speak, but no words come out.

He picks me up and seats me by the window. I stare out the window and see that the train is now traveling above ground. It is a beautiful fall day out. The foliage is remarkably colorful—yellow, bright orange. The deep red leaves especially enchant me.

I am staring at the rich colors when I feel a light tap on my shoulder. It's the little girl with the red hair. "Miss, I think you should get off here," she suggests.

I accept her suggestion.

As I step out of the train, the doors shut quickly, almost grabbing my foot. I jump toward the platform. Then, I look up in complete horror. The train is on fire. Red glowing flames melt the paint off the cars. I hear the high-pitched screaming of the children. They bang on the windows, their flesh slowly melting off their bones. The stench of burning hair and skin is in the air and there are bloody handprints on the windows.

The burning train slowly pulls out of the station. I sit on the platform floor, trying to figure out where I am.

The platform is completely desolate. A cold wind rushes through; small pieces of garbage fall onto the tracks. The sky now looks tranquil, its deep blue color patched by small white clouds.

I get up and brush the dirt off my clothes. As I lift my head, I see someone at the end of the platform. It's the man in the dark blue suit who was with me on the train.

He slowly walks toward me. He says, "You have to come with me. Don't worry."

I obediently follow him down the abandoned stairwell.

—Claudia Miranda

About this last piece, the author says, "I had this dream about two people, people I didn't know. The girl wasn't me and the boy wasn't anyone I'd ever gone out with, but the dream was very realistic yet mysterious about their relationship."

Notice how the atmosphere of the dream is both realistic and rather murky, as if everything was a little out of focus, as if no one can quite see clearly. Notice, too, how the tone of the story changes—just as a dream often does—near the end of the story.

Understood

I admit I was nervous. I had been waiting in this dreary bar for at least ten minutes. He was supposed to have been here four minutes ago. I knew what was coming. The music faded and left only the deep rhythmic tones of the bass ringing in my ears. He had been avoiding me.

I remember when we were on his street, slightly intoxicated. It was one of those winter nights. The wind was rough and we were both so cold. The sky was incredibly clear, for the city anyway. And we stood there in silence.

"I'm in love with you, you know," he blurted out. Where it came from I have no idea. "You know?" he repeated. I nodded my head. I knew. That was all that was said. Of course, the next day, he was unable to handle the situation.

"About the other night. . . ." His voice was wavering.

"Yeah?" I stared at him as he twisted his ring back and forth on his finger.

"Well, I wasn't in the best state of mind." Had it been anyone else I would have killed him, but with him it was different.

"Yes?" My voice was flat.

" . . . Not that I didn't mean what I said, or anything. Because . . . uh . . . well . . . I . . . I." He was looking around nervously, as though I was going to jump on him at any minute.

"Yes?" My voice tightened, my weariness turning to frustration.

"I sound like a prick." His body relaxed. He half smiled, searching my face for a reaction.

I stared at him a moment longer. "Yes," I said. I allowed him a smile. He smiled too—relief. That was the end of the conversation. He didn't like to bring it up. I knew. He knew. It was understood.

So he was in love with me, even though he didn't want to say it. I should have hated him for that, but I didn't. I accepted it. I don't know why. He couldn't deal very well with the situation. He tried, but I guess it didn't work. He had been avoiding me. I hadn't seen him for a week, and then he called.

So that left me to wait in this hole, and I knew what was coming. I knew what he was going to do. I should have hated him. I should have wanted to see him suffer a horrible, torturous, violent death. I didn't. I poured wax from one of the candles onto my finger and watched it harden. The candle flickered, and I looked up. He sat down with a swift, awkward movement and attempted to hold my hand. To humor him, I allowed this.

"Go to hell!" I wanted to scream. I wanted to hurt him. But I didn't. I couldn't. There was nothing to say.

"So," he mumbled. He was uncomfortable. I understood. I let some of my hair fall over my eyes, so he couldn't see what I was feeling. I gently pulled my hand away; I stirred my drink with my finger. I couldn't look at him. His soft, dark hair brushed against my face as he kissed my forehead. He lingered there.

Then, he was gone. And the pain was turning into anger. I threw the shot glass at the floor.

"Hey, lady, what do you think you're doing?" The bartender was angry.

"What does it look like I'm doing?" I took another glass and threw it at the floor.

232

"Look, lady, I don't know what your problem is but you need to calm down or get out. Know what I'm saying?" He was waiting for an answer. I took another glass and threw it, this time at the wall behind him.

"All right, lady, that's it. Either get out, or I call the cops." I stared at him blankly, trying to remember what was going on. He grabbed me by the arm and escorted me outside. "You crazy babes are all the same."

I started to cry. He was gone. He was gone, and I had let him hurt me. I let him see me. I let him get inside. And now he was gone.

"Lady, you gonna be OK?"

"Yeah. Hey, look, I'm sorry about what happened in there." I took out my wallet.

"Look, no, it's OK. We all have bad days." He wanted the money, though.

"Just take this, OK?" I handed him two twenties. I didn't know why. I didn't know anything. It was freezing outside and I wished I had brought a coat.

—Sarah Kelly

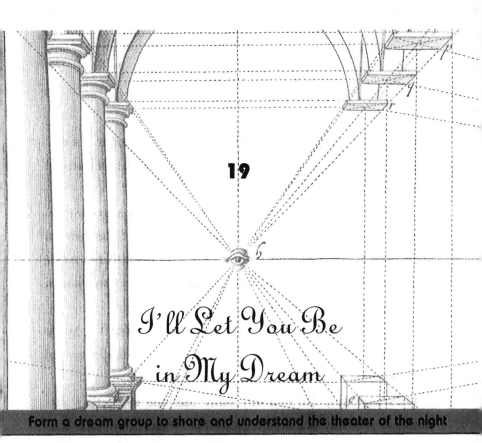

19

I'll Let You Be in My Dream

*I*f you saw a wacky movie last night would you (a) keep it to yourself, chuckling now and then at the parts that struck you as amusing or (b) phone your best friend and tell her all the funniest parts, even though your friend might not get the whole picture from your version?

Most of us would probably choose answer (b). Humans are such communicative creatures that we can't bear to keep pleasure (or pain, for that matter) to ourselves. We have to share it with our friends, family, or significant (and insignificant) others.

Well, many of you did see a wacky movie last night, the one that was showing for just a few moments in the darkened theater of your dreamworld. So, why not share it?

You may already have a friend or family member to whom you confide your dreams, but if you have found some of the material we've been talking about intriguing or if you feel that there are further adventures awaiting you in your quest into the unconscious, you might want to consider forming a dream group.

What is a dream group? What does it sound like? Yes, you're right! It's a group of people who come together to talk about—and make use of—their dreams.

Dream groups, like so many other odd and interesting phenomena, probably started in California, where they have been reported to be as common as pottery classes used to be. Their purposes may vary, but mostly they are formed with the idea of appreciating the complexities and wonder of dreams and making available to the group members their insights and potential for inspiration.

Deborah Jay Hillman, a cultural anthropologist who studies this grassroots dream movement reports that most dream groups range from three or four to as many as fifteen or twenty participants. There are artists' dream groups, lawyers' dream groups, women's dream groups. There are even dream groups for people involved in Alcoholics Anonymous!

Some dream groups explore the outer limits of the dream landscape, like psychic dreams. Other groups may try to utilize their dreams in a creative project—writing, painting, composing—based on the dreams of the group.

Most dream groups form because all the members want to pursue the elusive images of their night visions. As Hillman notes, most members of such groups assume that these images have meaning and that this meaning does not need a psychiatrist to unearth it.

Instead, Hillman observes, dream groups believe that the best route to dream insight is through discussions, brainstorming, and group exhortation to the dreamer himself to "unravel the many threads of meaning contained in the tapestry of a dream."

Does forming a dream group mean just getting a bunch of people together who will sit around and swap dreams? It does and it doesn't.

On the simplest level, that's just what you're after—a group of people who agree to gather at a particular time and in a particular place to share their dreams and their ideas about each other's dreams.

But whenever you are planning any group endeavor—sponsoring a dance, forming a club—you know it's going to be more complicated than that. Any new group needs to be thought through, and any group dealing with material as strange, personal, and filled with such potential for misunderstanding as dreams are needs to be approached with care.

After all, there are some people you may love dearly but would not want to share your dreams with—your cousin, for instance, who thinks anything to do with the brain is flaky stuff; the person whom you wish was more than just your friend and who regularly appears in your dreams; your brother, who tells you that everything is just about sex anyway.

And there are people who might be interested in dreams but are more interested in being the boss. A successful dream group—like a creative writing club or a band—requires that all members feel equally respected, get more or less equal time, and do not feel dominated by one member of the group. Of course, many (if not most) groups have one member who talks more than others do or who provides a lot of the energy—that's just human nature. But it's important for the group not to feel like Joe or Joann's dream group or even your dream group, but just a group of intelligent, curious seekers on the road to dream knowledge.

How should a dream group function? Most groups allow each member to be the focus of one meeting. Whoever is "it" that day describes a dream she has recently had—perhaps reading from a dream journal or just trying to recall it in as much detail as possible.

Then, members of the group try to make this dream "their own." They may say, "If that were my dream, I think it would be about being afraid of acting like an idiot. That giant dunce cap is really a cool image for worrying about being stupid."

Or they might say, "Whenever I dream about cats, it always seems to be about my sister. Does that make sense to you?"

Or "It could be about how you don't want to tell Rick that he's being really awful or that you're afraid he thinks you're awful."

Or whatever.

Each member of the group offers some off-the-top-of-his-head response to the dreamer's dream and then sits back and listens to what others say. The dreamer may want to write the ideas down or not. Then, when everyone is done, the dreamer gets to respond to what the group said. The dreamer might say, "The thing about the cat is interesting,

"All we see and seem is but a dream within a dream."

—*Edgar Allan Poe*

but I don't see Rick in this at all. But you know, now that I think of it, my brother and Rick were both acting like jerks last week. . . ."

The dreamer might say, "None of this really helps me right now. Guess I'll think about it later."

Or the dreamer might even say, "Why on earth did you think that? That's such a weird response!"

There are (at least) two important things to bear in mind here:

1. No one has the right to tell a dreamer what the dream means.

   Group members are there to offer feedback, suggestions, and associations. It's the dreamer's dream, and only the dreamer has the right to decide if an interpretation is correct.

2. Being defensive won't do anyone any good (though it's bound to happen now and then, especially when you first start doing this).

   The dreamer should try opening up to possibility and see whether any of the group members' suggestions click in any way—or even lead the dreamer to new thoughts of her own.

But dream groups do not need to be focused solely on the

interpretive aspect of dream knowledge. You may want to explore the dream telepathy section of this book with the group, work on lucid dreaming, act out childhood nightmares, or try to create a group project (a dream play, a dream sculpture, a dream mural) based on some or all of the group's dreams.

You may even want to experiment with shared dreaming. What is shared dreaming? In shared dreaming, a group of people agree to meet in their dreams by dreaming at the same time, in the same place, or by attempting to experience the same dream landscape—and then compare details after they awaken.

Earlier, we read examples of spontaneous mutual dreams—two people who know each other well and experience eerily similar dreams without discussing it beforehand. Such dreams may be examples of dream telepathy, or mere bizarre coincidence, or . . . something else. But in shared dreaming, dreamers try to make these dreams happen, "incubating" shared dream images, much the way lucid dreamers focus on attempting to attain the state of lucidity. In shared dreaming experiments, group members agree beforehand to try and dream about a particular dreamscape—a castle, say, or Mt. Everest, or a big, circular swimming pool in the middle of the desert (you can be as detailed as you like). The idea is to try to dream that you are in this place—or on the way there—with the other members of the group and see how close you can come to dreaming a similar dream.

You might also try to include a phrase or a word in your group dream, even a brief conversation. For example, you might agree to try and dream that wild geese fly by, regardless of where the dream is taking place, or that a blue bus drives by, or anything else. You might agree that you will try dreaming of yourselves in different roles or with different costumes or that you will shake hands in a certain way within the dream.

Like lucid dreaming or dream telepathy experiments, shared dreaming requires persistence, patience, an adventurous spirit, and, perhaps, a slightly weird sense of humor—just the sort of qualities shared by the people you've gathered together for your dream group!

Maybe.

But whether you choose to perform dream rap songs, work on dream choreography, explore dream premonitions, interpret one another's frightening (and absurd) dream imagery, or pursue the *Twilight Zone* world of shared dreaming, forming a dream group may be the next step you want to take on your journey.

Years ago, that cryptic folk poet Bob Dylan sang, "I'll let you be in my dream if I can be in yours."

So, open the door to your world, just a little, and let someone else you trust inside. Like music, poetry, or love, dreams may become richer, more magical, or more full of possibility the more they are shared!

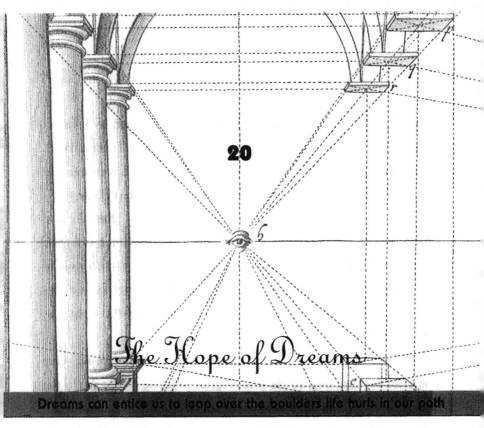

20

The Hope of Dreams

Dreams can entice us to leap over the boulders life hurls in our path

Almost 1,600 years ago, a Greek scholar named Synesius of Cyrene said, "Dreams, more than any other thing, entice us toward hope."

Does that sound strange?

Maybe not. After all, you've just read this book, so there's a pretty good chance that nothing you experience for a while will strike you as all that strange!

But, as this book reflects, most people tend to associate dreams with anxiety, absurdity, and improbability rather than with hope. They think of dreams as being filled with images of terror, truth, sex, even awe. But hope? Hope seems too quiet a sensation to associate with anything as tumultuous as the world of dreams.

But dreams flow in a way that our waking lives often do not. Dreams show us the boundaries we set around existence and then they say, "Leap! Fly over those walls!" They allow us to reconsider the route our lives are traveling and suggest—sometimes in a tiny voice, at other times with an ominous roar—that there may be other roads we ought to check out.

It's true that dreams can shake us to our very foundations, scare us until we can't bear to sleep for fear of what we might see in the night. But even as they wave their grotesque, bony fingers at us, dreams offer us the possibility of revising this frightening script, facing the monster, and turning it into a harmless, even laughable pile of rags.

In other words, dreams entice us toward a feeling that we might be able to overcome the boulders life hurls in our path—a feeling we might call hope.

Of course, not every monster is so easily dispatched—in waking life or in our dreams. There is such a thing as false hope, and there are plenty of boulders that can roll across our path against which even the richest, most enchanting inner life may prove powerless.

But dreams provide amusement and escape, even when we have reached dead ends. They can still open doors to creativity and self-knowledge, even if the real doors in this world slam shut in our faces.

So, maybe that's what old Synesius had in mind. And though the many worlds of dreaming are so complex that there can never truly be a final word, perhaps "hope" is a pretty good place to start-or stop.

Dream on!

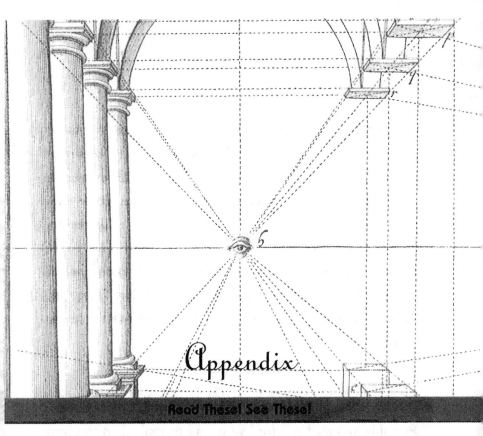

Appendix

*I*f you've ever cruised through the psychology or New Age section of a large bookstore, you know that there are about three zillion books about dreams out there. Some of them are turgid gobbledygook, and some of them are straightforward and clear. Some of them are insightful, and some of them are a little cheesy. Some of them are books I used as background for this book, and some of them are books I've never seen before.

I have not listed every possible book about dreams here, because that would be crazy; I haven't listed every book I referred to in the text here either, because some of those books are hard to find or close to unreadable. I have listed some of the most important books I referred to and some of the key books to know about in dream studies, as well as some dream art and literature—even some movies—that you might find intriguing, enlightening, bizarre, or just plain entertaining.

I've included a brief comment or two about this material, which really represents only one tiny stream of dream lore. Your task, then, is to jump in, splash around, and find which way the stream takes you.

Books to Read

Alice's Adventures in Wonderland by Lewis Carroll, Collier Books.
Probably, you read this (or had it read to you) when you were young, but this children's classic is also one of the great dream books. No one knows for sure whether Carroll actually dreamed any of this remarkable book, but it contains some of the most absurd and insightful observations about the nature of dreams and their relationship to reality ever written.

The Bloody Chamber by Angela Carter, Viking Penguin.
This book isn't really about dreams. It is a revisionist look at fairy tales and myths, but it is written with wonderfully

grotesque details, irony, and vivid understanding of the way in which day-to-day life resonates with dreamlike qualities.

Creative Dreaming by Patricia Garfield, Ballantine Books.

Garfield, a well-known dream researcher, describes many approaches to understanding our dreams, and this brief, commonsense book is one of the least ideological books about the value of dreams.

The Dreaming Brain by J. Allan Hobson, Basic Books.

Hobson, the controversial Harvard Medical School dream researcher, presents in this book his activation-synthesis model of dream interpretation in a difficult yet absorbing study of the chemistry of the brain. You may or may not agree with his ideas—and you may doze off during his long discussion of Freudian theory—but if you are seriously interested in dreams or the brain, you should take a look at this book.

Dreams by Carl Jung, Princeton University Press.

Unlike Freud, Jung never wrote a single book on his theories of dream interpretation. This book collects a number of essays and papers he wrote on dreams throughout his life. Some of it (especially the slightly weird stuff on alchemical symbolism in dreams) is hard to plow through, but there is a wealth of material here for serious dream students.

Dreams, Illusions, and Other Realities by Wendy Doniger
O'Flaherty, University of Chicago.
This is a dense and rather challenging book, but it contains a
wonderfully rich lode of material about the place dreams hold
in world mythology.

Dreamtime and Dreamwork edited by Stanley Krippner and
Jeremy P. Tarcher.
This is a terrific collection of essays and papers covering a wide
range of dream studies—from dream anthropology to psychic
phenomenon.

Freud for Beginners by Richard Appignanesi and Oscar Zarate,
Pantheon Books.
This is a funny idea—sort of an intellectual comic book—but
it's actually a good way to learn a little about Freud! A lot of
ideas packed into this short, entertaining volume.

Frida Kahlo by Hayden Herrera, Harper.
Kahlo, a modern Mexican painter, created some truly striking
dream paintings, especially her self-portraits. She has become
rather trendy in the past ten years or so, but that does not
diminish the power of her nightmarish images.

From the Teeth of Angels by Jonathan Carroll, Doubleday.

Carroll has a sort of cult following, and his novels, though sometimes irritating, are full of interesting ideas about fantasy, reality, and everything in between. This book uses dreams both as plot device and character insight and is well worth reading.

The Interpretation of Dreams by Sigmund Freud, Avon.

The most famous—and arguably most trying—book ever written about dream interpretation. Anyone who is seriously interested in dream studies should know about it. Just don't expect to have fun reading it.

Introducing Jung by Maggie Hyde and Michael McGuinness, Totem Books.

Similar to *Freud for Beginners*, this illustrated guide to Jung is a fine introduction to one of the more fascinating and elusive pioneers of dream psychology.

Let Your Body Interpret Your Dreams by Eugene T. Gendlin, Chiron Publications.

Despite a title that makes it sound like an article in the *Star*, Gendlin, who is a professor of psychology at the University of Chicago, offers a down-to-earth approach to dream interpretation.

A Little Course in Dreams by Robert Bosnak, Shambhala.

Bosnak is a Dutch Jungian dream analyst. This short book is a good introduction to some of the ways in which dream analysis is used by therapists and psychologists.

The Lottery and Other Stories by Shirley Jackson, Noonday Press.

You have probably run across "The Lottery" in some anthology; it's Jackson's most famous story, certainly. But just because you were forced to read her in eighth grade doesn't mean she's not any good. Her stories are almost all in the domestic-Kafka mode, moving with startling ease from the everyday to the bizarre, just as our dreams do.

Lucid Dreaming by Stephen LaBerge, Ballantine.

A serious yet easy-to-read book about contemporary dream studies, primarily focused on LaBerge's specialty—the facilitation, meaning, and implications of lucid dreaming.

Magritte by Suzi Gablik, Thames & Hudson.

Less famous yet arguably more influential than Dali, René Magritte's dream paintings are funny, startling, and important. This is a good introduction to his work.

Memories, Dreams, and Reflections by Carl Jung, Vintage.

Near the end of his life, Jung began this odd memoir. It describes many of the most important moments in his life—including his relationship with Freud and his revelations about dream interpretation—as well as some of his own dreams.

The Metamorphosis and Other Stories by Franz Kafka, Schocken.

Kafka, one of the most influential writers of the twentieth century, wrote stories and novels that are so remarkably nightmarish in tone that the expression "Kafkaesque" has passed into the language, used by people who have probably never read a word of his wonderful work. His stories are not exactly likable, but anyone interested in writing, the absurd nature of human experience, or the ways in which dreams can be used creatively should pay attention to him.

My Dreambook by Jack Kerouac, City Lights.

Kerouac, founder of the beat movement in American literature, wrote mostly realistic (if lyrical) novels about oddballs and misfits. But his poetry was highly influenced by Eastern mysticism, and this book of dreams shows him to have been quite immersed in the ways of the unconscious, too.

My Education: A Book of Dreams by William S. Burroughs,
Viking Press.

Burroughs, who recently died, was a sort of renegade novelist
and social satirist. He was a junkie, an expatriate, a friend, and
an inspiration to several generations of Bohemian/rebel writers,
musicians, and artists. This book is a bit of a memoir, a bit of a
journal, a bit of a dream log, and a bit of a nightmare. But it's
fascinating, as are many of his dark, nasty novels.

Night: Night Life, Night Language, Sleep, and Dreams by A.
Alvarez, W. W. Norton Company.

Alvarez is a literary scholar who uses this book partially to
describe his own experiences with nightmares and partially to
discuss the dream literature of such writers as Robert Louis
Stevenson and Samuel Taylor Coleridge.

On Dreams by Sigmund Freud, Norton.

Later in his career, Freud was persuaded that *The Interpretation
of Dreams* was too dense for most people to get through, so he
wrote this somewhat simpler book to further illustrate his theories. It's probably a better place to start your perusal of Freud.

One Hundred Years of Solitude by Gabriel Garcia Marquez,
Penguin.

Marquez, the Nobel Prize–winning novelist from Colombia, is
often described as a magical realist, and much of his writing has
an almost mythological quality to it—funny, melancholy, and
grotesque all at once. This novel has nothing much to say about
dreams except that it really is a dream, a dream of what the
world might be like if looked at with fresh eyes.

Our Dreaming Mind by Robert L. Van de Castle, Ballantine
Books.

This is one of the best books about dreaming out there, by a
man who has devoted most of his life to serious dream
research—but hasn't lost his sense of wonder about dreams.

The Oxford Book of Dreams edited by Stephen Brook, Oxford
Paperbacks.

This is a strange yet rather wonderful collection of literary quo-
tations and excerpts from journals, letters, and conversations
from some famous (and infamous) writers, all about dreams.

The Secret Life of Salvador Dali by Salvador Dali, Dover Books.

This memoir by the wildly eccentric surrealist painter describes some of his dreams and the influence dreams, Freud, and the unconscious had on his art and his life.

Sensual Dreaming by Dr. Gayle Delaney, Fawcett.

Your folks might not be so happy to see you bring this one back from the bookstore, but despite the slightly cheesy title and subject matter, Delaney is a serious dream researcher who offers a thoughtful look at the nature and meaning of sexual dreams.

Sixty Stories by Donald Barthelme, Viking Penguin.

Barthelme was a contemporary American short story writer whose work is witty, absurd, and hard to interpret, just like many dreams. Whether or not he actually used dreams for creative inspiration, the stories are often striking in their playful look at reality.

Sleep by J. Allan Hobson, Scientific American Library.

A simpler, illustrated view of some of Hobson's theories about the nature of consciousness and unconsciousness, this is a good place to start a serious investigation of the chemistry of the brain.

Surrealist Painting by Simon Wilson, Phaidon Press.

The word "surreal" has come to mean virtually any art or literature (or TV show, for that matter) that speaks in the language of dreams. But the original surrealists were mostly Parisian painters and poets of the early twentieth century who were greatly influenced by Freud. This is a good introduction to their work.

The Trial by Franz Kafka, Schocken.
This is one of the key dream novels of modern literature. OK, so it's a little depressing; read it anyway.

The Way of the Dream: Conversations on Jungian Dream Interpretation with Marie-Louise von Franz by Fraser Boa, Shambhala Publications, Inc.
Dr. von Franz, a friend and follower of Jung, has written numerous books about Jungian analysis, myth, archetypes, and so on. This book is actually a long conversation with her in which she discusses her insights into the psychology of dreams.

William Blake by Kathleen Raine, Thames and Hudson.
Much of Blake's poetry is rather oblique, but his strange, fragile, yet haunting artwork seems often to have been scooped right out of a dream and placed on the page. He was deeply influenced by dreams and visions, and the poetry shows it. This is the best introduction to his feverish creations.

A World of My Own: A Dream Diary by Graham Greene, Viking.

Although Greene, a well-loved British author who died in 1991, is not currently in vogue, his novels are full of the complexity and strangeness of the world. His dream diary, published in 1994, shows that he was keenly interested in that other world, equally complex and strange, that he found inspiring, intimidating, and liberating.

Films to See

An Andalusian Dog by Luis Bunuel.

This film, originally made in 1928, is based on Bunuel's dreams. It's completely grotesque and startling. Your local library may have a copy.

The Discreet Charm of the Bourgeoisie by Luis Bunuel.

This is one of Bunuel's last films. Bunuel was friends with painters Salvador Dali and Pablo Picasso. He was deeply influenced by the surrealist movement and by dream studies. This is a funny, satirical dream film. It can be found in video stores with a good foreign film section.

Psycho by Alfred Hitchcock.

You've probably seen this film, which is endlessly replayed on TV, but it has a remarkable nightmarish quality, as do many of

Hitchcock's films. If you've never seen the whole film, rent it! It's scary but has a surreal nature that can't quite be described—like the way the characters all seem to be dream doubles of each other. Hitchcock is thought of as a master of fright, but his films are deeply about the unconscious nature of human desire and fear.

Spellbound by Alfred Hitchcock.

A more blatant use of dream images exists in this film—especially Gregory Peck's dream sequence, which was designed by Salvador Dali. It was one of the first films to use Freudian psychology to help unravel a mystery.

Vertigo by Alfred Hitchcock.

Recently, this movie was rereleased. It's one of the best films ever, in this critic's view—a somewhat twisted and nightmarish view of human relations. It has nothing (and everything) to do with dreams but is filmed virtually as if it were a dream.

Bibliography

Appiganesi, Richard and Oscar Zarate. *Freud for Beginners*. New York: Pantheon, 1979.

Bosnak, Robert. *A Little Course in Dreams*. Boston: Shambhala Publications Inc., 1988.

Brook, Stephen, ed. *The Oxford Book of Dreams*. Oxford: Oxford University Press, 1987.

Dunne, J. W. *An Experiment with Time*. London: A & C Black, Ltd., 1927.

Fontana, David. *The Secret Language of Dreams*. San Francisco: Chronicle Books, 1994.

Freud, Sigmund. *On Dreams*. New York: Norton, 1952.

———. *The Interpretation of Dreams*. New York: Avon, 1965.

Garfield, Patricia. *Creative Dreaming*. New York: Ballantine, 1974.

Gendlin, Eugene T. *Let Your Body Interpret Your Dreams*. Wilmette, Illinois: Chiron Publications, 1986.

Hobson, J. Allan. *The Dreaming Brain*. New York: Basic, 1988.

Hyde, Maggie and Michael McGuinness. *Introducing Jung*.

Cambridge, Massachusetts: Totem Books, 1993.

Jung, Carl. *Dreams.* Princeton, New Jersey: Princeton University Press, 1974.

———. *Memories, Dreams, and Reflections.* New York: Vintage, 1989.

Jung, Carl and Marie-Louise von Franz, eds. *Man and His Symbols.* New York: Doubleday, 1964.

Krippner, Stanley, ed. *Dreamtime and Dreamwork.* New York: Jeremy P. Tarcher, 1990.

LaBerge, Stephen. *Lucid Dreaming.* New York: Ballantine, 1985.

Lewis, James R. *The Dream Encyclopedia.* Detroit: Visible Ink Press, 1995.

O'Flaherty, Wendy Doniger. *Dreams, Illusions, and Other Realities.* Chicago: University of Chicago Press, 1984.

Parker, Julia and Derek Parker. *The Secret World of Your Dreams.* New York: Perigee Books, 1991.

Van de Castle, Robert L. *Our Dreaming Mind.* New York: Ballantine, 1994.

von Franz, Marie-Louise and Fraser Boa. *The Way of the Dream.* Boston: Shambhala Publications Inc., 1994.

Zweig, Connie and Jeremiah Abrams, eds. *Meeting the Shadow.* Los Angeles: Jeremy P. Tarcher, 1991.